Aircraft

Kenneth Munson

Macdonald/Educational

Managing Editor Peter Usborne
Editors Su Swallow, Susan Ellis, Chris Milsome
Illustrators John Batchelor
              Brian Hiley
              William Hobson
              Frank Friend
              Tony Mitchell
              Jack Pelling
Illustrations consultant John W. Wood
Projects R. H. Warring
Picture research Marion Gain, Ann Usborne

Information and assistance were also given by
Thomas Foxworth, Michael Hooks, John W. R. Taylor,
The Port of New York Authority,
The Science Museum, London.

The Spitfire, pp 20, 21, is copyright "The Aeroplane"
The Phantom, pp 36, 37, is copyright McDonnell Douglas

First published 1971
Second edition 1974
Reprinted 1977
Macdonald Educational
Holywell House, Worship Street
London EC2A 2EN

contents

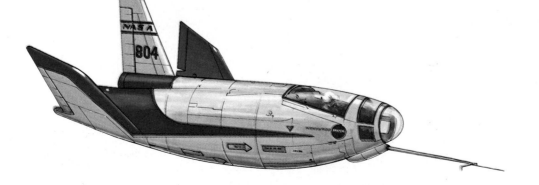

ISBN 0 356 03683 9

© Macdonald Educational Ltd 1971

Printed and bound by
New Interlitho, Milan, Italy

Aircraft the first steps

Leonardo helicopter design c. 1500

Montgolfier hot air balloon 1783

The Dream of Flight

For a long time, people thought that the best way for men to fly must be by copying birds. But none of the early attempts to make bird-like wings worked, and many died discovering that man is too weak and too heavy to fly like a bird. At last men began to think of using machines, not just muscles, for flying. Even then it took hundreds of years before the age-old dream of manned flight came true.

It was about seven hundred years ago that Roger Bacon, an English monk, suggested one of the first ideas for a flying machine, with flapping wings. More than two hundred years later, Leonardo da Vinci, a great genius, made sketches for a lot of machines which are now common, including aeroplanes and helicopters. Most of his machines were never built and many people continued to think that the secret of flying lay in imitating birds.

The first success

It was two French paper bag makers, Joseph and Etienne Montgolfier, who made the first aircraft to carry animals, and then men, off the ground. They built a huge paper-lined balloon which they filled with hot air, which rises because it is lighter than ordinary cool air. In 1783 a young scientist flew five and a half miles across Paris in one of these lighter-than-air balloons. But balloons had no power, and so could not be steered; they had to travel with the wind. It was nearly a hundred years before a steerable, powered airship flew.

Powered flight

Meanwhile, Sir George Cayley, an Englishman, made a heavier-than-air model glider, basically like a kite, which actually flew in 1804. This was the first proper fixed-wing aeroplane to fly. Cayley eventually built full-sized gliders many years later, in which boys and men rode. W. S. Henson made the first design for a complete powered aeroplane, although it never flew. Short hops in powered aeroplanes were made by Félix du Temple (1874), Alexander Mozhaisky (1884) and Clément Ader (1890).

Otto Lilienthal built many successful gliders and enormously improved aircraft design. His machines flew over two thousand times.

Leonardo da Vinci was a great scientist as well as a great artist. The sketch of a helicopter (above), made in about 1500, is one of his many designs for flying machines. It was never actually built.

The Montgolfier hot-air balloon (left), once called 'a cloud in a paper bag' first successfully lifted animals, and then a man, from the ground, in 1783. The miracle of flight by man had been achieved.

Cayley boy-lifter 1849

English baronet Sir George Cayley, the 'father of aeronautics', built the first aeroplane to fly—a model glider—in 1804. After his full-size 1849 glider (left), which could carry a boy, he developed one in which, in 1853, his coachman became the first man to fly in a heavier-than-air machine.

Lack of suitable engines held back early powered flying, and only short hop-flights could be made at first. Ader's steam-engined *Eole* (below) travelled about 150 feet through the air.

Ader Eole 1890

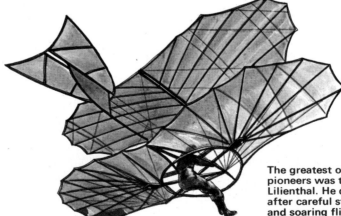

Lilienthal glider 1893

The greatest of the gliding pioneers was the German Otto Lilienthal. He designed his gliders after careful study of the gliding and soaring flight of birds. He controlled his gliders by altering the position of his body. In 1895 he made a biplane glider in which, in strong winds, he sometimes reached heights greater than the point from which he started.

First powered, controlled flight the 'Flyer'

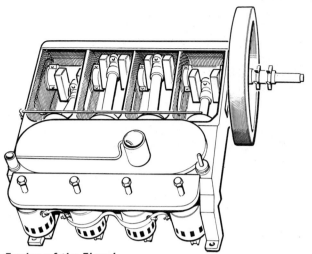

Engine of the Flyer I

The Wrights designed, and helped to build, the engine for their first *Flyer*. It was a four-cylinder, four-stroke petrol engine developing 12 horsepower. It weighed 179lb without its fuel.

The American brothers, Wilbur and Orville Wright, were given a toy helicopter by their father when they were boys. From that time on, they became fascinated by flying. But when they grew up, they started a bicycle manufacturing business, and even published a weekly newspaper, before turning again to their boyhood dreams of flying.

There were no published guides to propeller design. The Wrights had to make these too. They were remarkably efficient. The engine gearing enabled them to turn two-thirds of the engine's energy into forward thrust.

Controllable gliders

It was Otto Lilienthal's death in a glider crash in 1896 which led the American Wright brothers to start studying the problems of flight. They realised that it was Lilienthal's method of controlling his gliders by shifting his body around which caused his death. In their search for a safer method of control, they studied the way birds balance themselves in flight by twisting the tips of their wings.

By 1899, they had made a model biplane kite with a new system of 'wing warping' which enabled them to bend the free ends of the kite's wings as they wished. By doing this, they were able to steer the kite in different directions.

The next step was to build full-size gliders in which they flew and tried out their new invention.

Then they built a wind tunnel at their home in Dayton, Ohio, in which they tested more than two hundred model wings. After these experiments, they designed another full size glider, this time with a vertical rudder at the back connected with the wing warping mechanism.

The next problem was to find some means of driving their gliders through the air. All earlier attempts at powered flight had suffered from lack of light, powerful engines. The astonishing Wright brothers simply set about designing their own. They had to design their own propellers too.

At last a powered version of the Wrights' third glider was ready. The first trial flight at Kitty Hawk, North Carolina, on 14 December 1903, failed. But three days later, Orville took off

Upper main deck (wing) of 40ft span

Wing and strut bracing wires

Active wing-warping cable

Passive wing-warping cable

Wings covered with "Pride of the West" unbleached muslin fabric

and made the first powered, controlled flight, lasting twelve seconds. His plane had travelled 120ft.

The Wrights made three more flights the same day, always flying into a wind of a little over 20 mph. The last flight, piloted by Wilbur, lasted 59 seconds, covering 852ft over the ground.

These were the first controlled and sustained flights ever made by a powered aeroplane. At the Huffman Prairie, the Wrights made about a hundred flights in 1904 in their modified *Flyer II*. Because of the Prairie's small area, they often used a weight-and-derrick device to give them a catapult-style assisted take-off.

In 1905, the two brothers built their third—and first fully practical—aeroplane, the *Flyer III*. This could bank, turn and circle with ease. For the next two and a half years, they improved their designs, although they did no actual flying until shortly before a visit by Wilbur Wright to Europe in 1908.

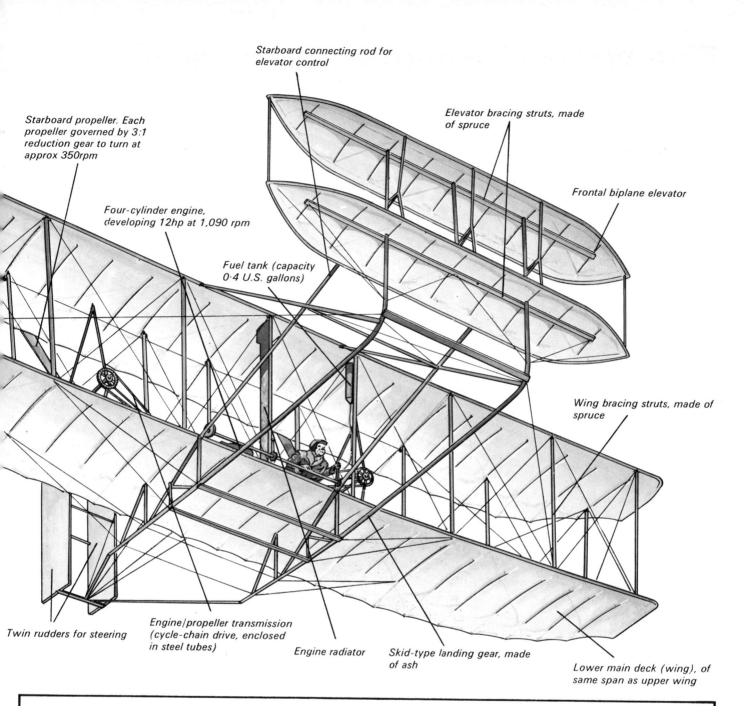

Starboard connecting rod for elevator control

Starboard propeller. Each propeller governed by 3:1 reduction gear to turn at approx 350rpm

Four-cylinder engine, developing 12hp at 1,090 rpm

Fuel tank (capacity 0·4 U.S. gallons)

Elevator bracing struts, made of spruce

Frontal biplane elevator

Wing bracing struts, made of spruce

Twin rudders for steering

Engine/propeller transmission (cycle-chain drive, enclosed in steel tubes)

Engine radiator

Skid-type landing gear, made of ash

Lower main deck (wing), of same span as upper wing

The Wrights' wing warping system

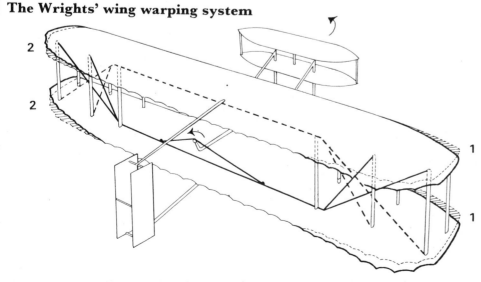

In the diagram on the left, the *Flyer's* wings are shown warped (twisted) for turning to the left. By moving the control stick to the left, one cable system pulled down the starboard, or right, rear wing-tips (1), while the other cable (shown dotted) pulled the port, or left, struts upward and raised the opposite tips (2). Moving the control column the other way gave opposite warp for a right-hand turn.

This system was based on the way birds control themselves in flight. It was the first really effective method of making an aeroplane 'bank' when turning. Since it required flexible wings, it was soon replaced in rigid-wing aeroplanes by a system of moveable surfaces known as 'ailerons'.

Decade of development pioneers 1906 to 1913

Alberto Santos-Dumont, a Brazilian, first became known for his airship flights around Paris at the beginning of this century. His tail-first box-kite, the *14 bis* (right), was his first powered aeroplane. In October-November 1906 it made the first successful flights by a European aircraft. Though only of short duration, they helped make Europe aware of the possibilities of flight.

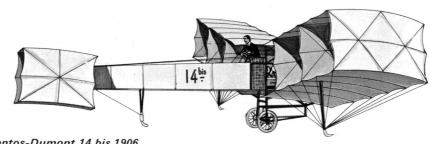

Santos-Dumont 14 bis 1906

From his first design, the 1908 bi-plane *June Bug* (right), American aviator Glenn Curtiss developed his prize-winning *Golden Flyer* of 1909 which flew at nearly 50mph. In 1911 Curtiss built America's first seaplane, and early in the following year he produced the first of several excellent flying boat designs. One of these, the *NC-4*, made the first west-to-east crossing of the North Atlantic (with stops en route) in May 1919.

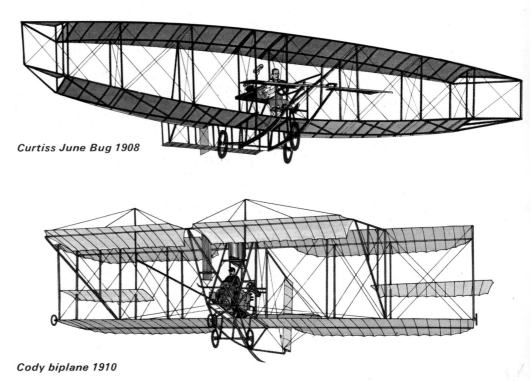

Curtiss June Bug 1908

The first sustained powered flight in Britain, of 1,390ft, was made at Farnborough on 16 October 1908 by an expatriate American, Samuel Franklin Cody, in his *British Army Aeroplane No. 1* (right), based broadly on the layout of the Wright biplane. A rule-of-thumb designer and a natural pilot, Cody (who later became a British citizen) won several competitions in his later aircraft before being killed when one crashed in August 1913.

Cody biplane 1910

Best speeds

1903 Wright Flyer I (US) 30mph
1904 Wright Flyer II (US) 40mph
1909 Blériot (Fr) 47¾mph
1910 Blériot (Fr) 68¼mph
1911 Nieuport (Fr) 82¾mph
1912 Deperdussin (Fr) 108¼mph
1913 Deperdussin (Fr) 126¼mph

Best distances

1903 Wright Flyer I (US) 852ft
1904 Wright Flyer II (US) 2¾ miles
1905 Wright Flyer III (US) 24¼ miles
1906 Santos-Dumont 14*bis* (Fr) 722ft
1907 Voisin-Farman I (Fr) 3,380ft
1908 Wright Flyer A (US) 78 miles
1909 H. Farman (Fr) 145½ miles
1910 M. Farman (Fr) 363½ miles
1911 Nieuport (Fr) 449¼ miles
1912 M. Farman (Fr) 628¼ miles
1913 H. Farman (Fr) 634½ miles

Flying becomes international

It was not until November 1907 that a European aeroplane flew for longer than a minute. By this time the Wrights' *Flyer* could stay up easily for forty-five minutes. Wilbur Wright visited Europe in 1908 and helped show the Europeans how to fly better.

In October 1908, the London Daily Mail newspaper offered £1,000 for the first man to fly across the English Channel. The prize was won in 1909 by the Frenchman Louis Blériot in a *Type XI* monoplane of his own design, flying from Calais to Dover in just over half an hour. Public excitement was tremendous. A month later, France held the world's first air meeting at Rheims. It attracted fliers from Britain, America and France and demonstrated how quickly Europe had learned the lessons of Wilbur Wright's visit only a year before. Records were broken daily.

Another important event in 1909 was the production of the first Gnome rotary engine. This became the first mass-produced aeroplane engine and gave the early aviators the light, reliable engine they needed. The Rheims meeting was the beginning of a whole series of national and international air competitions in the years before World War I. These meetings made it possible for pioneer aviators to exchange ideas with each other. Aircraft design and development made big advances in these early years, and by 1914 aviation had become a full-grown industry.

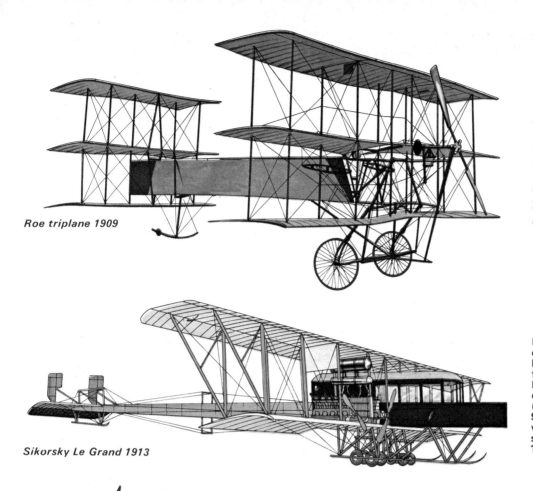

Roe triplane 1909

The Englishman, A.V. Roe, built a Wright-type biplane in 1908, but his first aeroplane to fly successfully was his 1909 triplane (left). It weighed 400lb when fitted with a 20hp engine, although its first flights were made with an engine of only 6hp. Roe's later designs included the *Avro 504* of 1913, one of the most famous aircraft of all time.

Sikorsky Le Grand 1913

Igor Sikorsky, known today as one of the greatest figures in helicopter engineering, built his first aeroplanes in Russia in 1909. His most outstanding pre-war design was the 1913 *Le Grand* (left), a four-engined giant with a 92ft wing span. An even larger version, the *Ilya Mourometz,* stayed airborne for 6½ hours in 1914, carrying six passengers.

Deperdussin Racer 1913

From 1911, monoplanes produced by the French company of Deperdussin were in the forefront of almost every important European and U.S. flying competition. The 1912-13 racing monoplanes, with their elegant moulded-plywood bodies and neatly-cowled rotary engines, were much more streamlined than earlier aeroplanes. In 1913 a 160hp Deperdussin racer shattered all previous world speed records by flying at nearly 127mph.

Blériot XI 1909

After experimenting with various aeroplane forms, Louis Blériot began to concentrate on developing a practical monoplane in 1906. Two such designs were displayed at the Paris air show two years later. One was the *Blériot XI* which, on 25 July 1909, became world-famous as the first aeroplane to fly the English Channel. The political and military repercussions of this flight were enormous.

The new weapon aircraft in World War I

When World War I broke out, very few aircraft on either side were robust enough for fighting in the air. One exception was the 90mph *Bristol Scout* (right).

By the end of the war, however, the Allies had several excellent fighters with twin synchronised machine-guns. Typical of these was the French *Spad XIII* (far right).

The *Albatros* fighters were the first two-gun German fighters, and reached their performance peak in the *D.III* version (right).

The outstanding German fighter of the war was the *Fokker D.VII* (far right), which had a superb performance even at altitudes above 16,000ft.

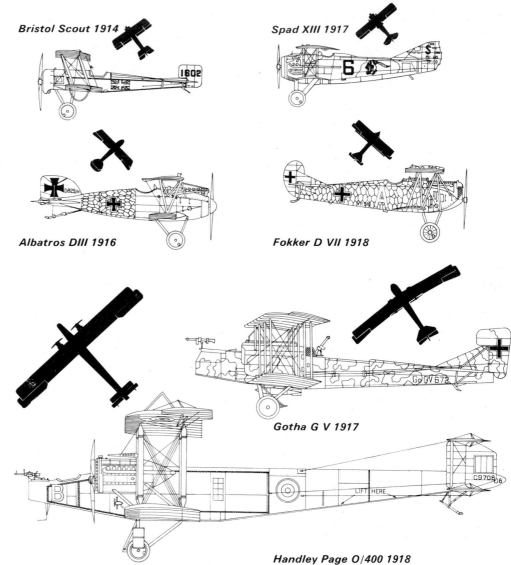

Bristol Scout 1914

Spad XIII 1917

Albatros DIII 1916

Fokker D VII 1918

Gotha G V 1917

Handley Page O/400 1918

The German *Gotha G.V* bomber (above right) could carry six 110lb bombs on a cross-channel raid against England.

The British *Handley Page* bombers were much larger than their German counterparts. The O/100 of 1916 could carry sixteen 112lb bombs internally; the O/400 of 1918 (below right) could lift a 1,650-pounder, the largest bomb to be used by Britain during the war.

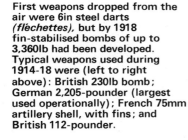

First weapons dropped from the air were 6in steel darts *(fléchettes)*, but by 1918 fin-stabilised bombs of up to 3,360lb had been developed. Typical weapons used during 1914-18 were (left to right above): British 230lb bomb; German 2,205-pounder (largest used operationally); French 75mm artillery shell, with fins; and British 112-pounder.

The first air war

When World War I broke out in 1914, the aeroplane was regarded by most commanders as having little use for fighting. Cavalry generals were afraid it would frighten their horses, and 90mph scout aircraft were thought 'dangerously fast'. There were very few bomber types in service, and fighters, as such, did not exist at all. But the value of aeroplanes for spying out the enemy's position from the air was obvious and more and more were used in this way. Inevitably aircraft from opposing sides sometimes met, and pilots had to start carrying arms to defend themselves.

From defence to attack was only a short step, and the first air war had begun in earnest. The war forced both sides to develop the first real fighters and bombers. By 1918, synchronised machine-guns replaced the carbines that were typical four years earlier; and bombs of up to 3,360lb had been developed—a far cry from the 20-pounders used to bring down the first Zeppelin from the air in 1915.

Successful dirigible (steerable) airships were pioneered in the late 19th and early 20th centuries. Germany's Count von Zeppelin took development a stage further by building huge rigid-frame airships, which were a great success as pre-war airliners. Zeppelins were much used for bombing during 1914-18, but losses were heavy.

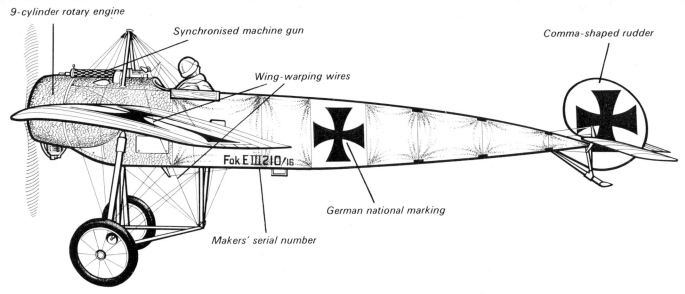

9-cylinder rotary engine

Synchronised machine gun

Comma-shaped rudder

Wing-warping wires

Fok E III 210/16

German national marking

Makers' serial number

The Fokker E III 1915

In March 1915 a French pilot was forced to land behind the German enemy's lines. His Morane-Saulnier monoplane carried a machine-gun which fired between propeller blades fitted with steel plates to deflect stray bullets. After seeing this plane, German engineers improved on the idea with an 'interrupter gear' which enabled a machine-gun to fire through the turning propeller without ever hitting the blades. This was carried by the *Fokker E-type* monoplanes, which became a formidable weapon against Allied aircrews, who had previously experienced forward-firing attacks only by pusher-propeller types of aircraft. In 1915-16 Fokker fighters shot down hundreds of Allied aircraft.

Technical data:

Engine: 100hp Oberursel U.I.
Wing span: 31ft 2¾in
Length: 23ft 11½in
Empty weight: 920lb
Gross weight: 1,400lb
Max. speed: 83mph
Time to 10,000ft: 28min
Operational ceiling: 11,500ft
Endurance: 2hr 45min

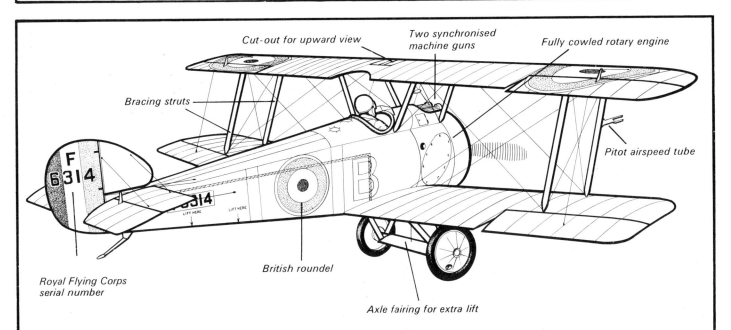

Cut-out for upward view

Two synchronised machine guns

Fully cowled rotary engine

Bracing struts

Pitot airspeed tube

British roundel

Royal Flying Corps serial number

Axle fairing for extra lift

The Sopwith Camel 1917

The *Sopwith Camel* was a typical late-war fighter design. It was developed from the earlier Sopwith Pup and Triplane fighters. It is supposed to have shot down more German aircraft than any other Allied fighter type. Its name is in fact a nickname derived from the 'hump' over the two syn-chronised Vickers guns mounted in front of the pilot. The standard F.1 Camel was used as both a day and a night fighter and for making ground attacks. Another version, the 2F.1, with shorter wings, was also produced. This operated in 1918 from aircraft carriers, battleships and cruisers of the British Navy.

Technical data:

Engine: 130hp Clerget 9B
Wing span: 28ft
Length: 18ft 9in
Empty weight: 929lb
Gross weight: 1,453lb
Max. speed: 113mph
Time to 10,000ft: 11min 45sec
Operational ceiling: 19,000ft
Endurance: 2hr 30min

S.E.5a fighting scout of World War I

Key to numbered parts
1 Aileron
2 Throttle
3 Radiator shuttle control
4 Elevator
5 Rudder
6 Rudder horn
7 Fabric-covered metal rudder
8 Tailplane incidence control gear
9 Skid (controlled with rudder)
10 Elevator horn
11 Typical fabric-covered wire-braced fuselage bay
12 Plywood decking
13 Aileron control quadrant
14 Starboard foot hole for boarding aircraft
15 Control column
16 Rudder bar
17 Bungee-sprung split axle
18 Aileron connecting wires
19 Oil tank
20 Main fuel tank
21 Radiator shutters' wheel control
22 Cylinder bank cover for Wolseley Viper engine
23 Radiator
24 Gravity-feed fuel tank
25 Vickers belt-fed ·303-inch machine gun
26 Ring-and-bead sight
27 Aldis telescopic sight
28 Foster mounting for Lewis gun
29 Lewis ·303-inch drum-fed machine gun
30 Double flying wires
31 Landing wires
32 Incidence bracing wires
33 Interplane struts

War forces the pace

Only thirteen years separate the design of the *S.E.5a* fighting scout from that of the original Wright *Flyer* illustrated on pages 4 and 5. Within that short time, pioneer designers and aviators had mastered the basic techniques and many of the problems of powered flight. They improved early methods of building aeroplanes, adapted the aeroplane for fighting, and established not only a new science, but a complete new industry to support it. The Wrights' 12 hp engine drove the original *Flyer* for half a mile at 30mph, at a height of a few feet; the *S.E.5a*, with a 200hp engine, could stay in the air for three hours, reach a height of 20,000ft and a speed of 120mph. It was made at the Royal Aircraft Factory at Farnborough, England, where Samuel Cody had made the first sustained flight in Britain only eight years earlier. The *S.E.5a* was typical of the fighters in service in 1917-18. It was built, as the diagram shows, with a wooden frame which had a plywood and fabric outer skin. It was controlled in the air by ailerons, elevators and rudder. The basic methods of aeroplane design and construction hardly changed in the next fifty years. The big changes were only in the materials.

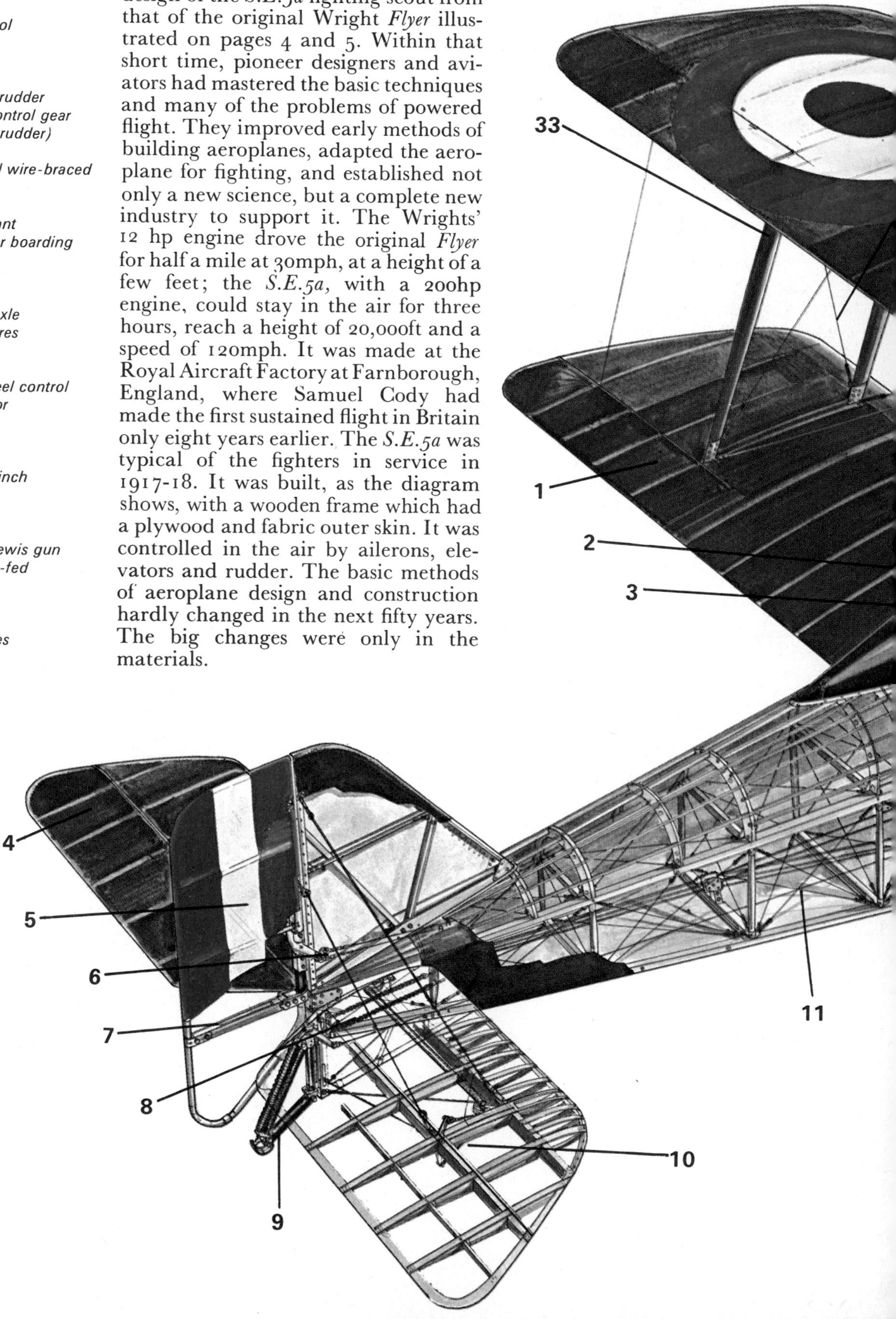

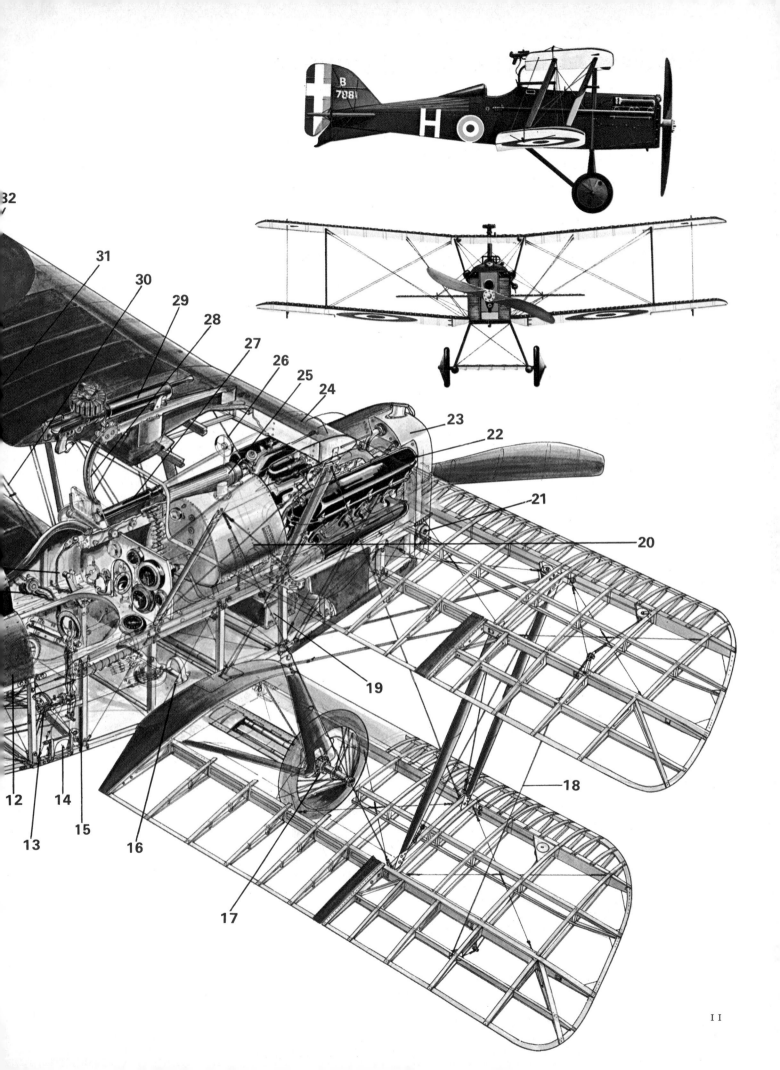

32

31

30

29

28

27

26

25

24

23

22

21

20

19

18

17

16

15

14

13

12

II

How an aeroplane flies the basic principles

The diagram on the right shows the four basic forces which act on an aeroplane. The lift of the wings has to counteract the downward gravitational pull of the aircraft's weight. The engine must push (or pull, in a propeller-driven aeroplane) the plane forwards with enough thrust to overcome the drag of the air. For stable flight, all four forces must pass through the same point.

Forces in flight

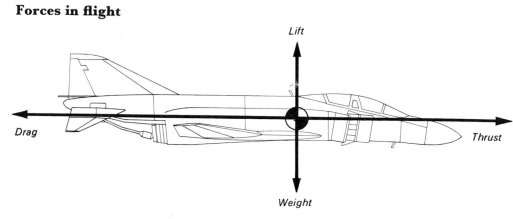

Lift

Drag

Thrust

Weight

The diagram above shows the cross section of a typical aeroplane wing. Notice the special curved shape, particularly on top of the wing. The front, or leading, edge of the wing is blunt.

As the wing travels quickly through the air, the air passing over the top of the wing has to go rather further because the top curve is longer. This creates a partial vacuum which tends to suck the wing upwards. The wing is also tilted at a small 'angle of attack'. This means that the air passing underneath the wings pushes up against the underside of the wing as it is deflected downwards.

Principles of flight

The laws of flight are the same today as they were for the first powered aircraft. The principles of flight are illustrated on these pages with a modern U.S. *Phantom* jet fighter, which has a jet engine to thrust it forwards, rather than a propeller like the Wrights' *Flyer*.

To fly, an aeroplane has to be travelling reasonably fast through the air. For every aeroplane, there is a speed below which it will stop flying properly and start falling to the ground. This is known as the 'stalling speed'.

In a powered aeroplane, the thrust which drives the aeroplane through the air comes from the engine and, on older planes, the propeller. As the plane passes through the air, the wings provide lift, as explained on the left. It

is the wings which support the plane in the air and prevent its weight making it fall to the ground.

One simple way to understand how a wing works is to hold something flat like a piece of cardboard or a paper plate, out of the window of a moving car. If you hold it quite flat, it will not tend to move either up or down.

But if you tip the front edge up slightly, with what is called, on aeroplanes, an angle of attack, you will immediately feel a pressure pushing up. If you could somehow hold out an object with a cross section similar to a wing, you would find that the upward pressure at the same angle was much stronger because of the partial vacuum created by the top surface shape sucking upwards.

Main control surfaces of the Phantom

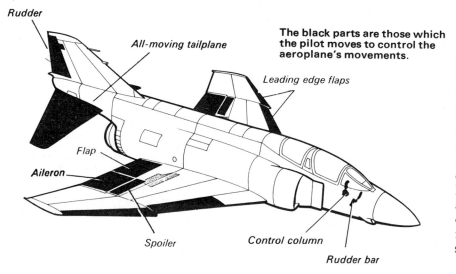

Rudder

All-moving tailplane

The black parts are those which the pilot moves to control the aeroplane's movements.

Leading edge flaps

Flap

Aileron

Spoiler

Control column

Rudder bar

The control surfaces

Obviously the pilot of an aeroplane has to be able to change direction, up and down and to either side. This is done by moving what are called the control surfaces. At the back of each wing there is an aileron, which can be moved up or down. These move in opposite directions and make the plane tip to the left or the right. This is called banking. At the rear of the aeroplane is the fin, which is upright, with a rudder which can be moved, like the rudder on a ship, to either side. Finally there are two horizontal surfaces at the rear. These are called the tailplane. Sometimes, as on the *Phantom*, the whole tailplane moves. On most planes, only the rear sections, known as the elevators, move.

Yawing

If the side area of an aeroplane is too small, the machine may start snaking dangerously from side to side, and get out of control (far left). The sides of the fuselage and the tail fin help prevent this movement, which is called 'yawing'. The smaller the side area of the fuselage, the bigger the fin has to be (left), to keep the total side area big enough.

Pitching

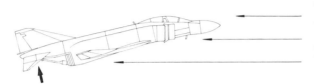

Another problem in designing aeroplanes is 'pitching', a switch-back movement (far left). The horizontal tail surfaces prevent this. As soon as the aeroplane starts to pitch, the airflow builds up against the bottom of the tailplane, if the tail has dropped (left), or the top, if the nose has dropped. This pushes the tail back to its original position, keeping the plane steady.

Rolling

If one wing of an aeroplane suddenly drops, the plane might 'roll' and start slipping sideways down to earth (far left). To stop this, wings usually bend upwards slightly. This is called dihedral. Then, if the plane slips, for instance, to the pilot's left (left), air pressure builds up under the left wing, pushing it up again and making the wings level again.

Stability and control

An aeroplane has to be designed so that it will fly on a straight and level course unless the pilot decides to change direction. This means that certain features have to be built in to prevent it suddenly going out of control when it passes through disturbances in the air. The diagrams explain how aeroplanes are designed to counteract the three dangerous movements known as yawing, pitching and rolling.

To change direction, the pilot uses the movable control surfaces, which press against the air rushing past. The rudder and the ailerons are used together to make the plane turn. The elevators make the tail drop or rise, and the plane then climbs or dives.

Climbing

Diving

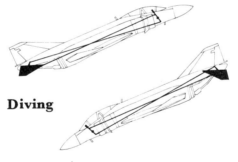

To make an aeroplane point upwards and climb, the pilot uses his tail control surfaces, or elevators. When these are deflected upwards (left, top picture), the airflow on top pushes the whole tail down, making the aeroplane point upwards. If the pilot wants to dive, he pushes his control column forwards, deflecting the elevators down. The air pressure is now underneath, pushing the tail up, and pointing the aeroplane downwards (lower picture on left).

Turning

Column straight

Rudder and aircraft straight

Moving the rudder to one side makes the air pressure push the whole tail in the opposite direction. This makes the nose of the aeroplane move to the same side as the rudder. But the plane will tend to 'skid' like a car unless it is also tipped, or banked, with the wing on the side to which it is turning being dipped, and the other raised. This is done by raising the 'inside' aileron or spoiler, and lowering the 'outside' one at the same time, as shown in the diagrams.

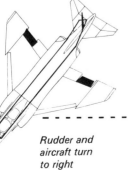

Rudder and aircraft turn to right

Column turned to right

The golden age of flying

FLYING FOR FUN

World War I convinced people that the aeroplane was a deadly weapon. But its usefulness and safety in peacetime still had to be proved.

After the war, some surviving bombers were converted to carry passengers, until the first proper airliners were built in the mid-1920s. Aeroplanes were also used for carrying mail.

But it was air 'circuses' which really made the public air-minded after World War I. Pilots toured the country, putting on shows of stunt flying and offering cheap joy-rides with war-surplus types of aeroplane such as the *Avro 504* and the *Curtiss Jenny*.

In 1925, the British de Havilland Aircraft Co produced the first of its famous *Moth* biplanes (right). This little aeroplane cost less than £600. It could be stored in a garage and towed to the nearest flying field behind the family car. It was very popular in private flying clubs and it helped the flying movement to spread rapidly throughout the British Commonwealth and other countries across the world. There are *Moths* still flying today, over forty years later.

DEATH OF THE AIRSHIP

The rigid airship, which was fairly common at the beginning of this century and during the early years of World War I, became popular again as a form of aerial transport in the late 1920s. Its supporters claimed that it was the most efficient method of carrying passengers over long distances. The huge German dirigible *Graf Zeppelin* (right) made a spectacular round-the-world trip of 21,500 miles in three weeks in 1929, flying the 7,000-mile stage from Friedrichshafen in Germany to Tokyo in Japan non-stop. Two British airships of the same period were the 700-foot *Vickers R 100*, which made a successful flight to Canada and back in the summer of 1929, and the government-sponsored *R 101*. But the *R 101*, prepared in too much of a hurry for a flight to India that October 1930, crashed in flames near Paris, killing many people. After this, Britain, France and America all stopped building airships. Germany continued to operate a successful trans-Atlantic service for some years with the *Hindenburg*. But in 1937, the *Hindenburg* exploded in flames at its mooring mast. The day of the rigid airship was over.

RECORDS AND RACING

During the years between
World Wars I & II, there was a
series of historic record breaking
flights. In 1919 John Alcock
and Arthur Whitten-Brown
made the first non-stop flight
across the Atlantic in a converted
bomber. In 1924, two single-
engined Douglas biplanes made
the first round-the-world flight.
In 1927, Charles Lindbergh flew
alone non-stop from New York to
Paris. In 1928, Charles Kingsford-
Smith flew 7,000 miles across the
Pacific. Many other great flights
followed.

Then there were the thrilling
competitive races. The Schneider
Trophy race was one of the most
famous, for seaplanes only.
The trophy was eventually won
outright by Great Britain after
three successive victories in 1927,
1929 and 1931 by the Supermarine
racers. The victor in 1931, the
Supermarine S.6B (left), was
flown by J. N. Boothman, at an
average speed of 340.08mph.

AIR TRAVEL

Air transport for passengers
developed quickly in the 1930s,
with a world-wide network of air
routes. Three American all-metal
monoplanes, the *Boeing 247*, the
Lockheed Electra and the *Douglas
DC-2*, revolutionised airliner
design.

Development in Europe was
slower but, in 1935, Imperial
Airways took the huge gamble of
ordering a fleet of 28 brand-new
'C' class flying boats. These
became famous for their speed and
comfort but they had one great
disadvantage. With a full load of
passengers, they could not quite
fly from Europe to America.

One curious solution to this
problem was the 1938 pick-a-back
Short-Mayo Composite aircraft
(left). *Maia*, the lower aircraft,
made the take-off. The smaller
Mercury was launched in mid-air
with full fuel tanks for the trans-
Atlantic journey. But in-flight
refuelling soon enabled the
ordinary *'C' class* flying boats to
make a conventional crossing. In
1939 British and American flying
boats started regular two-way
services.

Hannibal safety and luxury in the air

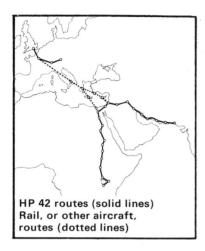

HP 42 routes (solid lines)
Rail, or other aircraft,
routes (dotted lines)

When Imperial Airways was formed in 1924, 124 of the 178 seats available in its fleet of 14 aircraft were in Handley-Page airliners. In 1928 the airline bought eight new *HP 42s* for £21,000 each: four London-to-Cairo *HP 42Ws* (*Heracles, Horatius, Hengist* and *Helena*) seating 38 passengers, and four longer-range 24-seat *HP 42Es* (*Hannibal, Horsa, Hanno* and *Hadrian*) for routes from Cairo to Africa and India.

The four 550hp Bristol Jupiter engines, each driving a huge 11ft 3½in four-blade propeller, were placed well clear of the passenger cabins to reduce interior noise and give travellers a really good view from the large windows. The *HP 42s* had a 130ft wing span and cruised at about 100mph. Their automatic wing slots, which made them very stable even at low speeds, meant they could operate easily from small airfields.

From 1931 to 1939 they flew throughout Europe and to Africa and India without a single passenger being killed. *Heracles* alone flew 1¼ million miles and carried 95,000 passengers. No wonder that the *HP 42* was called "not an aeroplane but a legend".

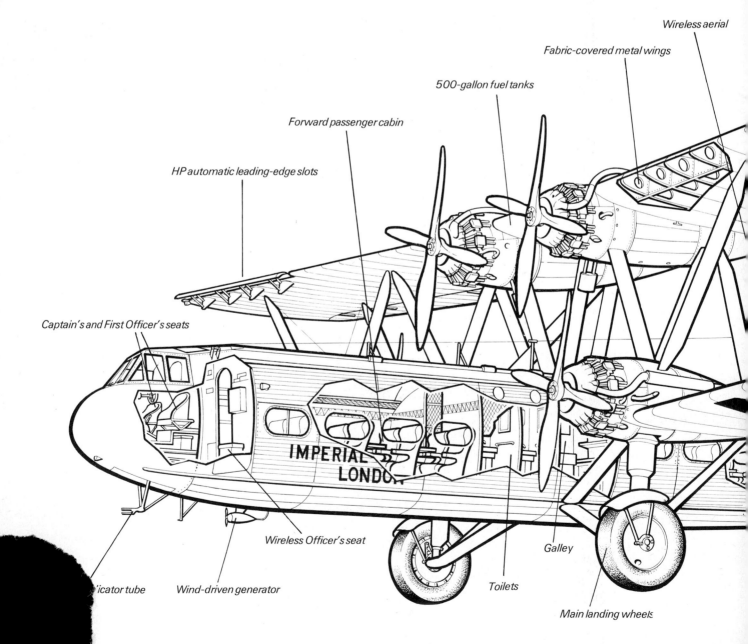

Wireless aerial

Fabric-covered metal wings

500-gallon fuel tanks

Forward passenger cabin

HP automatic leading-edge slots

Captain's and First Officer's seats

IMPERIAL
LONDON

Wireless Officer's seat

...icator tube

Wind-driven generator

Galley

Toilets

Main landing wheels

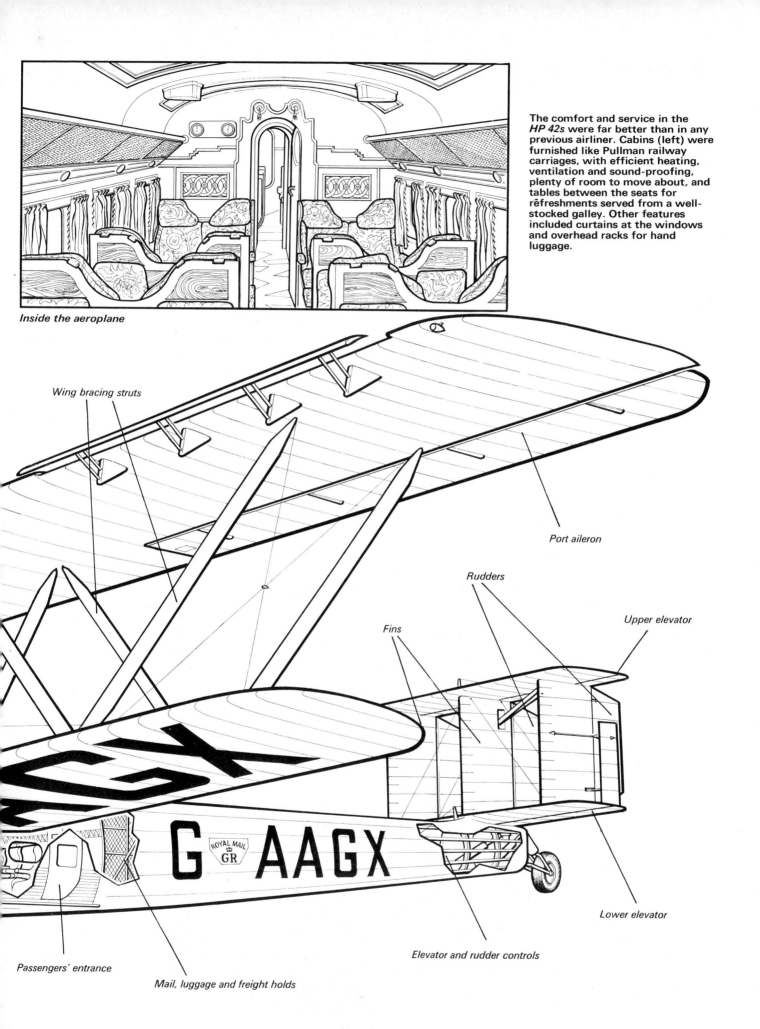

Inside the aeroplane

The comfort and service in the *HP 42s* were far better than in any previous airliner. Cabins (left) were furnished like Pullman railway carriages, with efficient heating, ventilation and sound-proofing, plenty of room to move about, and tables between the seats for rêfreshments served from a well-stocked galley. Other features included curtains at the windows and overhead racks for hand luggage.

Wing bracing struts

Port aileron

Rudders

Fins

Upper elevator

G AAGX

ROYAL MAIL
GR

Lower elevator

Elevator and rudder controls

Passengers' entrance

Mail, luggage and freight holds

Converted from a pre-war airliner, the *Focke-Wulf Fw 200 Condor* (right) became Germany's most feared naval reconnaissance bomber. It worked with packs of German submarines (U-boats), attacking convoys carrying vital food and military supplies.

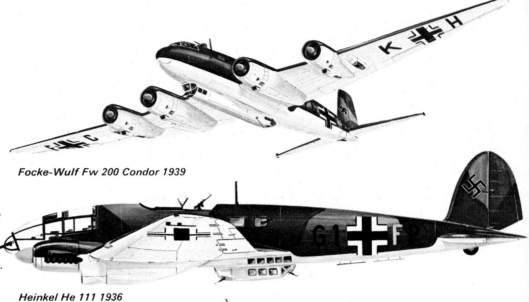

Focke-Wulf Fw 200 Condor 1939

The German *Heinkel He 111's* (right) first operational service was in the 1936–39 Spanish Civil War, where it had little opposition. In the Second World War it carried more guns and had fighters to protect it. When it became out of date as a bomber, it was used for dropping torpedoes and minelaying.

Heinkel He 111 1936

The main threat to the British air force in the Battle of Britain was the 'E' version of the *Messerschmitt Bf 109* fighter (right). One of the most widely-built warplanes of all time, this 1935 design reached its wartime peak in the 430mph *Bf 109G*, commonly known as the 'Gustav'. This had a 1,800hp engine.

Messerschmitt Bf 109 1936

The most adaptable German warplane of the Second World War was the *Junkers Ju 88.* It was originally designed as a bomber, but later, like the British *Mosquito*, it performed many other roles. These included dive-bombing, torpedo-dropping, mine-laying, photo-reconnaissance, day and night fighting (right), ground attack and training. Its bomb load was 4,000lb.

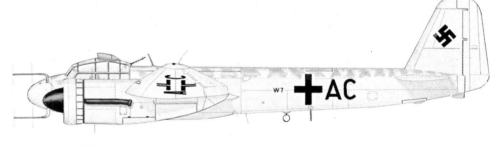

Junkers Ju 88 1939

V1 missile 1944

The first of the German 'secret weapons' was the *V1* missile (above). It was soon nicknamed the 'doodlebug'. It did a lot of damage to England during the last half of 1944 before its launching sites could be destroyed. The *V1* carried a 1,870lb high explosive warhead in its nose.

'Axis' air forces

In World War II, Germany and her allies, Italy and Japan, were known as Axis powers. Germany started the war with the most powerful air force in Europe. Because this air force (the *Luftwaffe*) was much stronger than those of her enemies, the German land armies were able to advance quickly across Europe.

The Battle of Britain was its first big defeat, although the bombing of Britain continued for some time afterwards. But the *Luftwaffe* was gradually forced back on the defensive. It was stretched even further after Hitler's unsuccessful invasion of Russia in 1941. Bombing of German aircraft factories and railways from 1943 onwards slowed down the production of new aircraft. In the end,

the *Luftwaffe* ran out of fuel completely.

The Italian air force was strong in numbers, and its aircraft were well designed. But, with a few notable exceptions, the performance of the Italian planes was not as good as that of German and Allied aeroplanes.

Japan also entered the war with powerful army and naval air forces, but these were soon spread so thinly over the huge land and sea areas in south-east Asia captured by the Japanese ground forces that production of new aircraft could not keep up with the numbers shot down by the Allies. The Japanese aircraft carrier force suffered particularly heavy losses in 1942-43. Even the suicide pilots, who dived deliberately to their death, could not keep off final defeat.

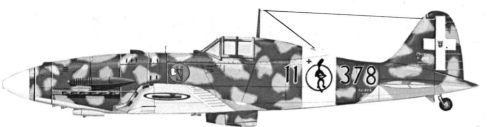

Macchi C.202 Folgore 1941

The best Italian fighter was the *Macchi C.202 Folgore* (left). Its predecessor, the *C.200 Saetta* of 1937, was an excellent design, but its performance was poor because of its bulky low-powered 840hp radial engine. The *Folgore,* produced by putting a 1,200hp German Daimler-Benz inline engine in the same airframe, weighed half a ton more but was over 50mph faster.

Kawanishi H6K 'Mavis' 1938

Japan needed long-range aircraft to patrol between the many groups of islands in the Pacific. Typical of these was the *Kawanishi H6K* 'Mavis' flying boat (left), which had a range of over 3,000 miles.

Mitsubishi G4M 'Betty' 1941

Ohka in launch position

Ohka piloted bomb 1945

One of the Japanese Navy's chief medium bombers was the *Mitsubishi G4M* 'Betty' (above left), which could carry 2,200lb of bombs, or a torpedo, over a 2,000-mile range; but with over a thousand gallons of fuel in unarmoured wing tanks it was easy to destroy. 'Betty' is best remembered as mother-plane for the *Ohka* piloted bomb (left)—the only operational Japanese aircraft specially designed for suicide attacks. This was launched in the air from under the *G4M's* bomb bay (far left), gliding to its target and then using its rocket engine for a 620mph death dive.

Nakajima Ki-84 'Frank' 1943

Japanese fighter pilots usually preferred light aircraft like the 'Zero' and 'Oscar' of the early war years. But they soon learnt the value of armour plate and self-sealing fuel tanks, as used in the *Nakajima Ki-84* 'Frank' (left), one of the best Japanese Army fighters of the war.

Mitsubishi J2M 'Jack' 1943

The *Mitsubishi J2M* 'Jack' (left), built specially for intercepting high-flying Allied bombers, was plagued by early development troubles. Fortunately for the enemies of the Japanese, its engines were in short supply and less than five hundred were built.

Battle of Britain the Spitfire

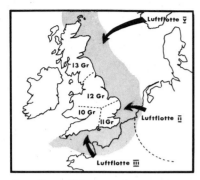

Location of German air groups (Luftflotte) during Battle and areas of Britain defended by four RAF groups. British radar range shaded.

Hitler's first defeat

At the beginning of World War II, the German army smashed through Poland, Czechoslovakia, France, Belgium and Holland at incredible speed. The British air force attempted to help keep the invaders out of France, but it quickly lost nearly a quarter of all its modern aircraft.

The British decided that France could not be held, and that they must save what aircraft they had left to defend themselves in case the Germans attacked England.

It was not long before German bombers started pounding southern England, to prepare the way for an invasion by the army. But this time the small British air force, relying heavily on its *Spitfire* and *Hurricane* fighters, put up a fantastic fight. German bombers suffered terrible losses.

The Germans then started to send their long-range fighter, the *Messerschmitt Bf 110*, as escort for their bombers to try to protect them from the onslaughts of the British fighters. But the British pilots, who stayed by their machines 24 hours a day, ready to 'scramble' into the air at a minute's notice, found they could still out-fly the German fighters. The British had

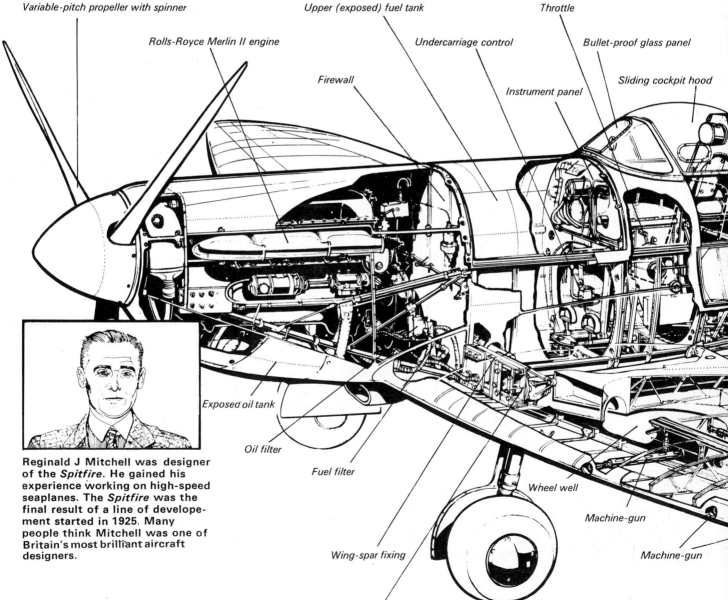

Reginald J Mitchell was designer of the *Spitfire*. He gained his experience working on high-speed seaplanes. The *Spitfire* was the final result of a line of developement started in 1925. Many people think Mitchell was one of Britain's most brilliant aircraft designers.

Variable-pitch propeller with spinner

Rolls-Royce Merlin II engine

Firewall

Upper (exposed) fuel tank

Undercarriage control

Instrument panel

Throttle

Bullet-proof glass panel

Sliding cockpit hood

Exposed oil tank

Oil filter

Fuel filter

Wheel well

Machine-gun

Machine-gun

Wing-spar fixing

Undercarriage hinge-bracket fixing to spar

managed to install a new electronic detection system, radar, along the east and south coasts of the island. So they knew in advance when the German planes were coming, and could be ready to meet them.

Eventually the Germans had to send *Messerschmitt Bf 109* fighters, which had a much shorter range, to protect the *Bf 110s*, which were protecting the bombers! This worked quite well, but the German fighters were fighting much further from their bases than the British, and could not stay up for long before they had to turn back for home.

For three months the British pilots fought a desperate battle for their country against the much bigger German air force. At last the German dictator, Hitler, realised he had met his match, and gave up his attempt to invade England. The German war machine had been beaten for the first time.

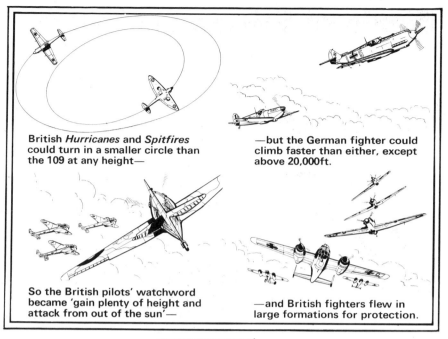

British *Hurricanes* and *Spitfires* could turn in a smaller circle than the 109 at any height—

—but the German fighter could climb faster than either, except above 20,000ft.

So the British pilots' watchword became 'gain plenty of height and attack from out of the sun'—

—and British fighters flew in large formations for protection.

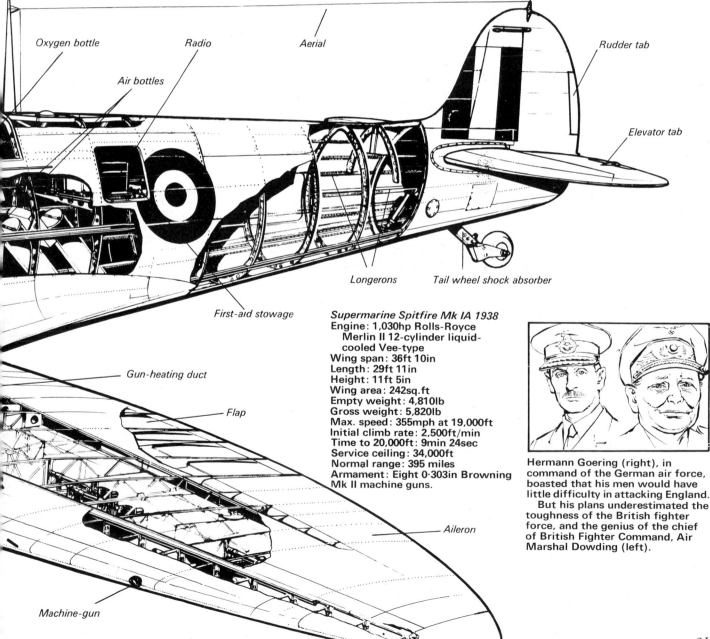

Oxygen bottle

Radio

Aerial

Rudder tab

Air bottles

Elevator tab

Longerons

Tail wheel shock absorber

First-aid stowage

Gun-heating duct

Flap

Supermarine Spitfire Mk IA 1938
Engine: 1,030hp Rolls-Royce
  Merlin II 12-cylinder liquid-
  cooled Vee-type
Wing span: 36ft 10in
Length: 29ft 11in
Height: 11ft 5in
Wing area: 242sq.ft
Empty weight: 4,810lb
Gross weight: 5,820lb
Max. speed: 355mph at 19,000ft
Initial climb rate: 2,500ft/min
Time to 20,000ft: 9min 24sec
Service ceiling: 34,000ft
Normal range: 395 miles
Armament: Eight 0·303in Browning
Mk II machine guns.

Aileron

Machine-gun

Hermann Goering (right), in command of the German air force, boasted that his men would have little difficulty in attacking England.
  But his plans underestimated the toughness of the British fighter force, and the genius of the chief of British Fighter Command, Air Marshal Dowding (left).

World War II Allied fighters and bombers

The American *P-51 Mustang* (right), one of the greatest fighters ever built, was actually designed to British specifications, and powered by a British Rolls-Royce Merlin engine. By the end of the war, more than 15,000 had been built. The final version could fly at 465mph.

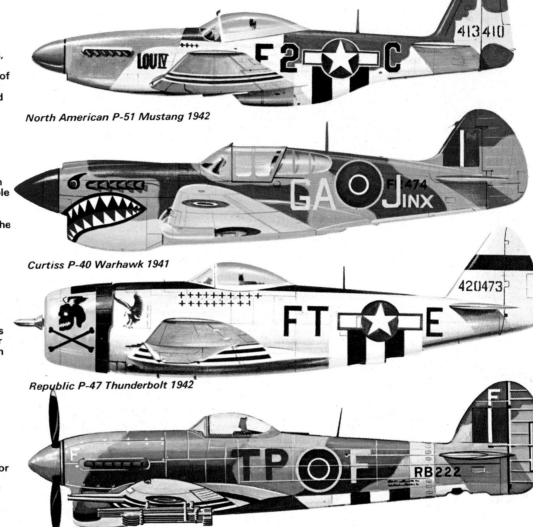

North American P-51 Mustang 1942

The *P-40 Warhawk* (right) was an unspectacular but highly adaptable American fighter. These planes fought on nearly every front, particularly in North Africa and the Pacific, and were used by the British, US, Canadian and Australian air forces.

Curtiss P-40 Warhawk 1941

The *P-47 Thunderbolt* (right) was used as a fighter, fighter-bomber and rocket projectile carrier from 1942 onwards. When it was first introduced, it was the biggest single-seater of its time.

Republic P-47 Thunderbolt 1942

The British *Hawker Typhoon* (right) was originally designed for intercepting enemy aircraft. It turned out not to be particularly effective in this role, but it was then equipped with underwing bombs and rockets, and became one of the war's most deadly train-busters and low-level attack aircraft.

Hawker Typhoon 1941

Until World War 2, the basic weapons carried by aircraft were the gun and the bomb. The rocket projectile, used experimentally in 1914-18, came into prominence from about 1942. It quickly proved effective for attacking tanks, supply trains and other ground targets.

Fighters

When America joined the war, Allied air strength increased enormously, and the balance of power shifted dramatically against the Germans and their 'Axis'. A new breed of American fighter aircraft joined Britain's struggling *Spitfires* and *Hurricanes*.

Most of the fighters built during and after World War I were twin-gunned biplanes. With World War II, monoplanes quickly took over from biplanes. Fighter armaments steadily improved. Machine guns were replaced by larger cannons, and later in the war many fighters also carried bombs or rockets.

The remarkable electronic 'eye', radar, developed by the British before the outbreak of war, was adapted for use in aircraft, enabling them to find and shoot down enemies and attack ground targets in the dark.

Piston engines improved tremendously, making possible aeroplanes which flew much much higher than before and at speeds up to fifty per cent faster than the typical fighter of the first year of the war.

Each side kept up a constant struggle to keep one step ahead of the other in building better and faster aeroplanes. Some designs, like the *Defiant*, were rushed out too quickly, and suffered severe teething troubles. Others, such as the *Mosquito*, proved to be even more effective than expected.

Towards the end of the war, naval fighters, based on huge aircraft-carrying ships, became an important weapon.

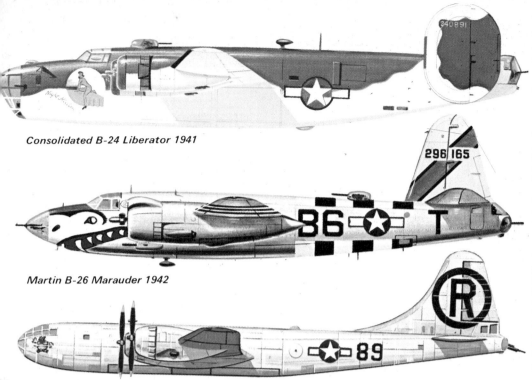

Consolidated B-24 Liberator 1941

Martin B-26 Marauder 1942

Boeing B-29 Superfortress 1943

Avro Lancaster Mk III 'dam buster' 1942

The American *Consolidated B-24 Liberator* (left) made hundreds of daylight bombing raids across Europe. Because of its very long range, it was also extremely effective on the long distance raids in the south-west Pacific.

When it first came into service, the *Martin B-26 Marauder* (left) suffered so many losses that it used to be called the 'widow maker'. But its performance improved tremendously, and it was used more than almost any other bomber in the war. It carried 11 guns, and a 5,200lb bomb-load.

The huge *Boeing B-29 Super-fortress* bomber (left) came into the war fairly late. It was used in the Pacific against Japan, and was the first US bomber which could fly the very long distances necessary to bomb Japan itself. *Superfortresses* dropped the two terrible atomic bombs which finally brought the Japanese to surrender.

The British *Lancaster* bomber (left) was used in a famous raid against the great German Moehne and Eder dams. It carried a drum-shaped bomb underneath its fuselage, specially designed to skip over the water, roll down the dam wall and explode below the level of the water.

Bombers

Seven main types of four-engined heavy bomber were used by the Allies during World War II—Britain's *Stirling*, *Halifax* and *Lancaster*, America's *Fortress*, *Superfortress* and *Liberator*, and the Russian *Pe-8*. Their size enabled them to carry huge fuel loads for long-range flying, and heavy bomb loads, completely inside their fuselages. During the second half of the war, radar bombing aids enabled very accurate 'pin-point' attacks to be made, and the use of 4,000-lb and 8,000-lb bombs became common. Britain developed a huge 22,000-lb bomb called 'Grand Slam', which was too big to fit in any existing bomber and could be carried only by specially adapted Lancasters.

In Europe the main bombing attacks against Germany were made at night by the three British 'heavies', and in daylight by the American *Fortresses* and *Liberators*. Against the Japanese, *Liberators* and *Superfortresses* were the main types used.

The war was brought to an end by the two small but terribly destructive atomic bombs dropped on Japan by American *Superfortresses*. Oddly enough, the four-engined bomber was not much used by the Axis powers. Italy's *Piaggio P.108* was used only in small numbers, while Germany's only important four-engined bomber—the *Heinkel 177*—was a failure, and Japan used no heavy bombers at all. Germany, however, produced the only operational jet bomber—the *Arado 234*—although this was not in the 'heavy' class.

23

Finding the way aircraft navigation

When Henry Farman made the world's first cross-country flight in 1909, he found his way by flying low over landmarks on the ground below. Blériot was out of sight of land for one-third of his pioneering flight across the English Channel, and did not even have a compass to guide him.

Before a flight, early pilots used to draw a line on their maps between their starting and finishing points. They then made a note of landmarks on the way, such as large towns, railway lines or rivers. They had to rely on their eyesight and a clock to tell them if they were on course. This method imposed great strain on the pilot. It did not always work in bad weather, low cloud or at night.

Rotating loop aerials (right) were an early method of direction finding (D/F), which could fix the position of an aircraft by picking up signals from radio transmitters on the ground (A and B). A rotating loop aerial indicated, on a scale inside the cockpit, the exact angle ($a°$ or $β°$) between the heading of the aircraft and the transmitter. The pilot then plotted these two directions on his map, and his position was where the lines met. The lower picture shows the D/F loop fairing, which was usually placed on top of the aircraft behind the crew cabin.

The position of an aircraft can be calculated by using a sextant (right), a very accurate clock and a set of tables showing the known position of stars and planets above the earth at any time. By looking through the sextant at a given star, a navigator can measure its angle in the sky. He can then read off his direction from a point directly beneath the star. Readings from two stars will give him an exact 'fix'.

This aircraft (B) is flying from X to Y. If it headed directly towards Y, the wind would blow it off course. To prevent this it must head off course against the wind at an angle ($a°$). The navigator finds this angle by using A (his latest 'fix'), and the known speed and direction of the wind and of his aircraft through the air, to plot the lines AC and AB on his map. Joining C and B then gives him the angle he wants.

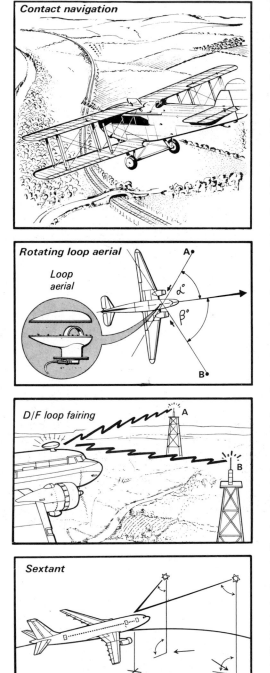

Contact navigation

Rotating loop aerial

Loop aerial

D/F loop fairing

Sextant

Calculated position of aircraft

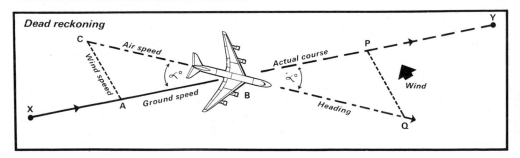

Dead reckoning

Air speed

Wind speed

Ground speed

Actual course

Heading

Wind

Early air navigation

Pilots of airliners soon after World War I often had to follow railway lines or rivers. As air travel distances increased, the need for something more precise than this so-called 'contact' navigation became vital.

As time went on, aerial navigation relied more and more on instruments. The simplest of these is the compass. The navigator works out from a map the direction or 'bearing' from his starting point to the place to which he wants to fly. He can read this bearing off his compass. This will show him the actual direction to his destination. But he cannot simply fly in this direction because the wind will blow him off course.

'Dead reckoning' and 'fixes'

It is a fairly simple matter to calculate the actual direction in which to fly, if the speed and direction of the wind, and of the aircraft, are known. These are given by weather reports from the ground and by the airspeed indicator and compass in the aircraft. The diagram below explains how the 'dead reckoning' method of navigation works.

A navigator must check his actual position at regular intervals, and position 'fixes' can be taken in several ways. A landmark is the simplest of all. But a suitable landmark may often not be visible. Sometimes a sextant can be used to work out a position from the stars. But as flying has developed, more and more ground radio stations have been set up as aids to air navigation. The signals from these, the position of which a navigator will have marked on his map, act almost like lighthouses for an aircraft. The direction of (and, nowadays, the distance to) these stations can be read off instruments in the aircraft as soon as their signals are received.

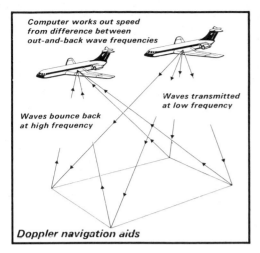

Computer works out speed from difference between out-and-back wave frequencies

Waves transmitted at low frequency

Waves bounce back at high frequency

Doppler navigation aids

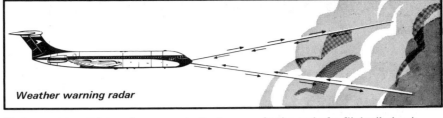

Weather warning radar

Radar equipment (above) can now indicate positions of clouds ahead on a cathode ray tube in the cockpit of an aircraft. The same radar equipment can also be used to 'map' the ground below.

The Doppler navigation aid (left) sends down high-speed radio beams from any height. These 'bounce' back to the aircraft. A computer aboard the aircraft calculates true ground speed and drift.

At the end of a flight (below), pilot and navigator have several aids to guide them accurately in to the airport. Landmarks, such as towns and rivers, provide visual 'fixes'. As the aircraft approaches the airport, it flies into an air traffic control lane, In constant communication with the control tower at the airport. It may have to circle in a 'stack' until a runway is free for landing.

Modern navigation

Before World War II, radio stations transmitted signals on Low and Medium Frequency bands. In bad conditions, these signals were often distorted or even lost. During the war, Very High Frequency (VHF) radio was developed. This worked almost without interference even in the worst weather. Now, Distance Measuring Equipment (DME) also indicates the distance from a radio transmitter, which means that a navigator can work out a 'fix' from the signals of only one transmitter if necessary.

Today, airliners are usually fitted with a pair of so-called 'Automatic Direction Finders' (ADF's), one tuned in to a radio station ahead and one behind. Continuous bearings towards the radio stations are shown on dials in the cockpit, while DME equipment shows the distances to the stations on another set of dials.

Radar, also developed during World War II, is another important navigational aid. Beams are transmitted from the aircraft, and bounce back when they meet solid objects or even raindrops. Radar apparatus can be used to give precise height above ground, especially over mountains, and can detect bad weather far ahead, enabling a pilot to alter course, if necessary, well in advance.

Modern Doppler navigation systems can measure speed and drift from the shift in the frequency of waves bounced off the ground. Doppler can be used with an airborne computer, which will work out 'dead reckoning' calculations automatically from information fed into it.

The latest airliners have fully automatic 'inertial' guidance systems. These record all changes in the speed and direction of an aircraft automatically. This data is fed into a computer which calculates exact positions without relying on ground aids at all.

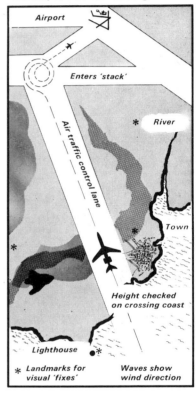

Airport

Enters 'stack'

* River

Air traffic control lane

* Town

Height checked on crossing coast

Lighthouse

*

* Landmarks for visual 'fixes'

Waves show wind direction

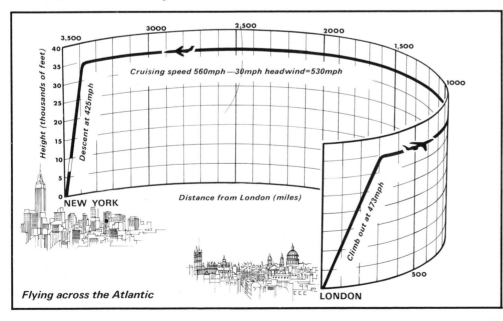

Flying across the Atlantic

Cruising speed 560mph—30mph headwind=530mph

Descent at 425mph

Climb out at 473mph

NEW YORK

LONDON

Distance from London (miles)

Height (thousands of feet)

The graph on the left shows the pattern of a typical trans-Atlantic passenger flight from London to New York. By the time the aircraft has climbed to its correct cruising height of 35,000 feet, it has already covered nearly one-tenth of the distance before levelling out to continue on its westbound heading. Over the Atlantic it will have to fly against headwinds which reduce its effective speed. (On the return trip eastwards, of course, these winds are behind it and add to its speed, so reducing journey time.) Just over 100 miles from the airport at New York, it begins its descent in readiness to join the 'stack' of aircraft waiting to land and disembark their passengers.

Development of the jet

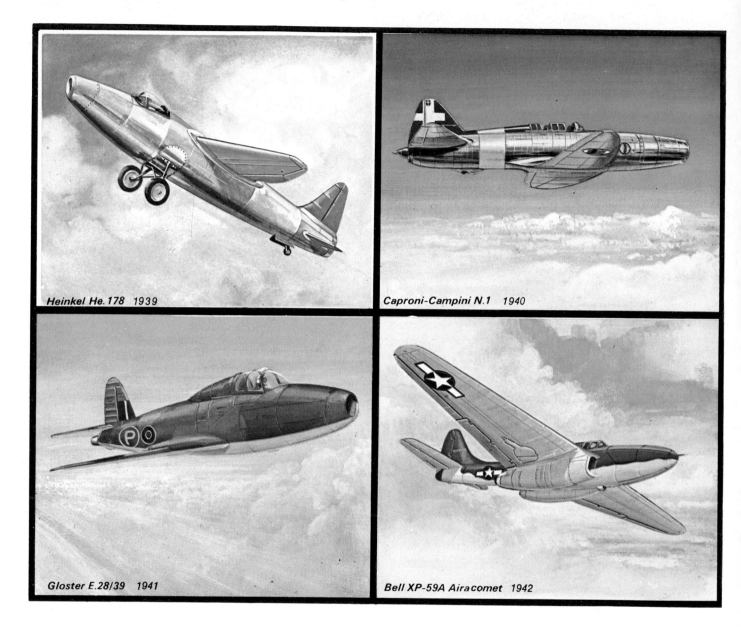

Heinkel He.178 1939

Caproni-Campini N.1 1940

Gloster E.28/39 1941

Bell XP-59A Airacomet 1942

The *Heinkel 178* (top left) was the first turbojet-powered aircraft in the world to fly, on 27 August 1939. It had a Heinkel HeS 3B jet engine, developed by Pabst von Ohain.

The Italian *Caproni-Campini N.1* (top right) became the second jet aeroplane to fly in 1940. It was the first jet to fly across-country, in November 1941, although it only flew then at an average speed of 130mph.

The *Gloster E.28/39* test aircraft was a British aeroplane powered by one of Frank Whittle's early engines. It first flew in May 1941.

The American *Bell XP-59A Aira-comet* first flew in October 1942. It used a GE-1-A turbojet engine, which was developed from a version of the Englishman Frank Whittle's engines.

The beginnings of jet aircraft

The first ideas for jet aircraft engines were made as early as 1910. Articles about gas-turbine jet engines were published in Britain in the late 1920s. The two men who finally invented practical gas-turbine engines were Frank Whittle in Britain (who had patented his ideas in 1930) and Pabst von Ohain in Germany. These two did their work quite separately, but their first experimental engines were made to work within a month of each other, in 1937.

The German engine was developed more quickly and was put into the world's first jet aeroplane to fly in 1939. This was nearly two years before the first British jet aeroplane flew, but the British machine was definitely the better of the two. Even on its early flights in 1941, the little *Gloster E.28/39* could fly almost as fast as the piston-engined fighters of the time, on about half their power. Later, with a more powerful Whittle engine, it reached 466mph. Meanwhile, a Whittle engine was supplied to the US at the request of the US Army Chief of Staff and an American firm, General Electric, developed the engines installed in the first American jet, the *Bell XP-59A*.

During World War II, the Germans used the jet-driven V1 flying bomb, two jet fighters (*Heinkel 162* and *Messerschmitt 262*) and a jet bomber (*Arado 244*). Japan also made some experimental jet aircraft. But the Allies only used the *Gloster Meteor* in action.

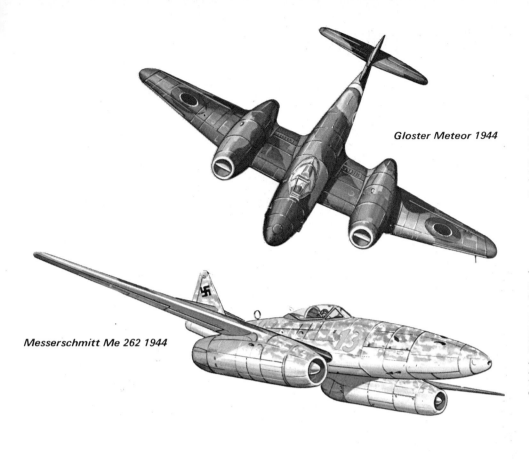

Gloster Meteor 1944

Work on the British *Gloster Meteor* began in 1940. It entered service in 1944. Its first task was the interception of the *V1* flying bombs over southern England. In 1945, *Meteors,* the only Allied operational jet fighters of the war, were sent to join the 2nd Allied Tactical Air Force fighting in Germany.

Messerschmitt Me 262 1944

The twin-jet *Messerschmitt 262* became operational with the German air force in 1944, after six years of development and delay. During the year that it was in service, it never engaged the British *Meteor* in air-to-air combat, but several were shot down by Allied *Mustang, Spitfire, Tempest* and *Thunderbolt* piston-engined fighters which, although slower, could turn inside the jet.

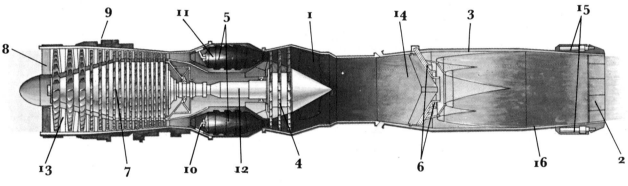

How a jet engine works

In a jet engine, air is sucked in and passes through a compressor, which pumps it at pressure into the combustion chambers. Here it mixes with vaporised fuel and is ignited. This produces very hot gases. Still at high pressure, these pass through the turbine blades and turn them with just enough force to drive the compressor. Then the remaining gases shoot out at high speed through the exhaust nozzle. The explosively expanding gases inside the engine push in all directions. Obviously these are only free to escape through the nozzle at the back, and it is the reaction against this escaping force that propels the aeroplane forwards. The 'kick' of a gun when it is fired is produced in the same way, only in a gun the explosion only happens once whereas in a jet engine it is continuous. The advantages of jet engines over piston engines are that, pound for pound of weight, they give more power, and are more economical to run. Having fewer working (i.e. moving) parts, they are also more reliable and need less maintenance.

From the pilot's point of view, a jet aircraft has fewer engine instruments. He must check to be sure his engines are working properly, but he is mainly concerned with pressure and temperature. With piston engines, he also has to watch revolutions per minute, oil pressure, fuel flow and mixture ratio, and other facts, all needing space on his instrument panel and regular checking.

Key to numbered parts

1. Exhaust gases
2. Variable area nozzle
3. External cooling air
4. Three-stage turbine
5. Combustion chambers
6. Fuel injectors
7. Compressor blades
8. Air intake
9. Sixteen-stage compressor
10. Fuel inlet
11. Vaporised fuel
12. Shaft connecting compressor and turbine
13. Stator blades
14. Afterburner
15. Nozzle actuators
16. Jet pipe

Jet airliners high speed passenger transport

The British *de Havilland Comet 1* (right), first flown in 1949, was the world's first jet airliner. It went into service with the British airline, BOAC, in 1952. In 1954 a number of Comets crashed, killing a large number of passengers. The metal fatigue which caused the crashes meant that Comets had to be withdrawn, and the improved *Comet 4* did not come into service until 1958.

Russia's *Tupolev Tu-104* (right), first flown 1955, was adapted from a military design, the Tu-16 bomber. Its original 50 seats were increased to 70 in the *Tu-104A* and 100 in the *Tu-104B* of 1959. These three models continued in operation until the late 1960s.

The jet airliner revolution

The jet revolutionised airliners as well as warplanes. After World War II, airline traffic increased quickly, and it was natural that the jet should be adapted for passenger aircraft.

The first jet airliner into service was the British *Comet 1*, which carried its first fare-paying passengers in 1952. This gave the British a long lead over their overseas competitors. But in 1954 they received a serious setback when a series of *Comet 1*'s crashed. A structural weakness was found in the aircraft, and it had to be withdrawn.

Meanwhile the Americans had developed a new generation of much larger jet airliners. The new US *Boeing 707's* and *Douglas DC-8's* were eagerly snapped up in large numbers by the world's airlines, replacing the traditional propeller-driven airliners.

A new fashion was also introduced in 1955 by France's *Caravelle*, with two engines at the back.

The subsonic jet airliners now flying vary greatly in size. The most significant recent newcomer has been the huge *Boeing 747* 'jumbo jet', which entered service in 1970.

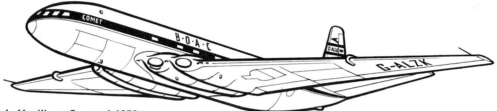

de Havilland Comet 1 1952

Tupolev Tu-104 1956

Boeing 747 1970

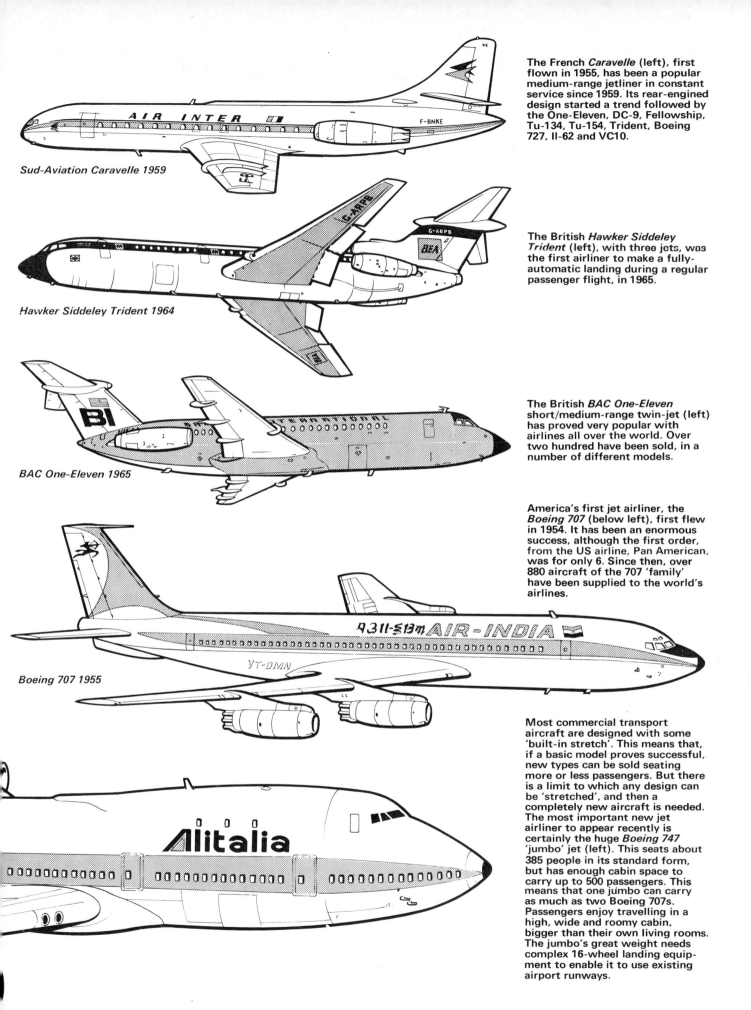

The French *Caravelle* (left), first flown in 1955, has been a popular medium-range jetliner in constant service since 1959. Its rear-engined design started a trend followed by the One-Eleven, DC-9, Fellowship, Tu-134, Tu-154, Trident, Boeing 727, Il-62 and VC10.

Sud-Aviation Caravelle 1959

The British *Hawker Siddeley Trident* (left), with three jets, was the first airliner to make a fully-automatic landing during a regular passenger flight, in 1965.

Hawker Siddeley Trident 1964

The British *BAC One-Eleven* short/medium-range twin-jet (left) has proved very popular with airlines all over the world. Over two hundred have been sold, in a number of different models.

BAC One-Eleven 1965

America's first jet airliner, the *Boeing 707* (below left), first flew in 1954. It has been an enormous success, although the first order, from the US airline, Pan American, was for only 6. Since then, over 880 aircraft of the 707 'family' have been supplied to the world's airlines.

Boeing 707 1955

Most commercial transport aircraft are designed with some 'built-in stretch'. This means that, if a basic model proves successful, new types can be sold seating more or less passengers. But there is a limit to which any design can be 'stretched', and then a completely new aircraft is needed. The most important new jet airliner to appear recently is certainly the huge *Boeing 747* 'jumbo' jet (left). This seats about 385 people in its standard form, but has enough cabin space to carry up to 500 passengers. This means that one jumbo can carry as much as two Boeing 707s. Passengers enjoy travelling in a high, wide and roomy cabin, bigger than their own living rooms. The jumbo's great weight needs complex 16-wheel landing equipment to enable it to use existing airport runways.

Airport

At any airport, airliners depend upon numerous ground support services and vehicles before leaving on a flight. For example, this tractor is one of many types used to tow them to and from overhauls in the maintenance hangars.

'Turnaround' servicing between flights keeps many people busy, cleaning out the cabin and toilets, re-stocking the galleys with fresh water and supplies of food and drinks for the next trip. Truck-mounted galley servicing containers like this one (above) can put directly aboard several tons at a time.

Today's airliners have enormous fuel capacities—nearly 50,000 gallons for a 747. This can be pumped aboard, at upwards of 500 gallons a minute, from huge fuelling bowsers or from smaller vehicles (above) drawing their supply via a hydrant beneath the airfield.

KEY
(1) Departing aircraft taking off
(2) Arriving aircraft about to land
(3) Control tower
(4) Approach lights
(5) Taxiway
(6) Landed aircraft on taxiway to terminal building
(7) International Arrivals Building
(8-14) Airline 'satellite' terminals
(8) Pan American Airways
    Aeroflot
    Air Afrique
    Nigeria Airways
(9) Northwest Airlines
    Braniff International
    Northeast Airlines
    Finnair
(10) Eastern Airlines
    Mohawk Airlines
    Aeronaves de Mexico
(11) United Air Lines
    Delta Airlines
    Japan Air Lines
(12) American Airlines
    Olympic Airways
    New York Airways (helicopters)
    Air Commuter Services
(13) BOAC
(14) Trans World Airlines
    British West Indian Airways
(15) Covered walkways for embarking/disembarking passengers
(16) Car parks
(17) Main highway in and out of airport
(18) Maintenance hangars
(19) Aircraft parked on apron for turnround
(20) Fuel storage area
(21) Departing aircraft taxiing to runway for take-off

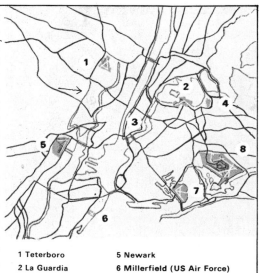

New York is one of the busiest areas in the world for air traffic. All air movements are controlled by the Port of New York Authority. The map shows the main airports round New York for which PNYA is responsible: the international one, named after President Kennedy, La Guardia and Newark municipal airports, the Manhattan Island heliport, the light aircraft field at Teterboro, and various military bases. New York Airways flies a helicopter link between Kennedy and the city centre, and a network of multilane highways and expressways (shown in red) connects the different airports. Such links are essential if the advantages of fast air travel between countries are not to be lost by slow surface travel between airports and cities.

1 Teterboro
2 La Guardia
3 Heliport
4 Flushing
5 Newark
6 Millerfield (US Air Force)
7 Floyd Bennett Field (US Navy)
8 John F. Kennedy International

Baggage loaders for most inter-continental airliners can carry five or six tons of luggage at a time, though even these need to make several trips before filling the 44-ton maximum baggage capacity of a jumbo jet.

The method of getting passengers from the departure lounge to their aircraft varies from airport to airport—by bus, tunnel or overground walkway. One interesting approach is the use of 'jetways', telescopic 'fingers' extending from the terminal building itself.

Handling traffic at Kennedy airport

At a busy international airport, air-liners arrive and depart every few minutes of the day and night. As each new plane-load leaves (1) there are others waiting to take its place. When incoming airliners (2) enter an airport's air traffic control area, they are 'stacked' a safe distance away, circling in a descending spiral until it is their turn to land. As they come in to land on the runway, they may be 'talked down' by the men in the airport control tower (3), with the added help of approach lights (4) at night or in bad weather. When they have landed, special markings (5) or lights down the centre of the runway show which taxiway each aircraft must follow (6). At Kennedy International Airport in New York they will taxi to either the International Arrivals Building (7) or to one of the surrounding terminals (8-14). Here the passengers disembark into the building, collect their baggage, and pass through Customs and Immigration. Car parks (16) are close by, and the traveller can drive off along one of the main high-ways (17) out of the airport. Mean-while, the aircraft may move to a maintenance area (18) for overhaul, or stay on the apron (19) to be refuelled and restocked. Fuel supplies are kept at special storage areas (20), away from the busy airport centre. When the aircraft has been refuelled, and re-stocked, it is ready to take on its next load and taxi out (21) to take off again.

For the passenger's safety, nothing is left to chance. All airports have standing by, at instant readiness, a fleet of runway clearance vehicles, fire appliances, crash tenders and ambulances, so that no time is lost in getting help to the spot if there is an accident.

Supersonic transport

Fast-flying jet aircraft have to pass through the so-called 'sound barrier', reached when the aircraft's speed nears the speed of sound. This is 761mph at sea level, but 99mph slower above 35,000ft, which is where modern jets usually fly. The speed of sound is often called 'Mach 1'; 'Mach 2' is twice the speed of sound, and so on. You can find out an aircraft's Mach number if you divide its speed in mph by:

$$761 - 2.784 \left(\frac{\text{altitude in feet}}{1,000} \right)$$

At any speed, an aircraft creates a pressure wave ahead of it which travels at the speed of sound and 'warns' the air in front to move out of its way. When the aeroplane itself nears sonic speed, the air has no time to do this, and so builds up into shock waves along the plane's nose, wings, fuselage and tail. These can subject the airframe to severe stresses. Supersonic aircraft must have specially-designed shapes to pass through the shock 'barrier' unharmed.

The shock waves themselves cannot be eliminated. Once the aircraft is flying faster than sound they spread out behind it in a cone-shaped pattern. The lower portion of these waves continues travelling until it reaches the ground, where it creates a sudden rise and fall in atmospheric pressure which is heard as the 'sonic boom'. The amount of noise depends on the plane's size, its height and speed above the ground, and the weather below. At its worst, it can cause damage to buildings, so supersonic airliners will probably have to fly below the speed of sound over land.

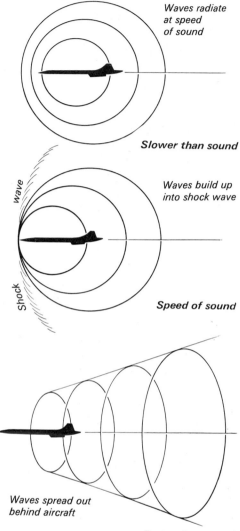

Waves radiate at speed of sound

Slower than sound

Waves build up into shock wave

Speed of sound

Waves spread out behind aircraft

Faster than sound

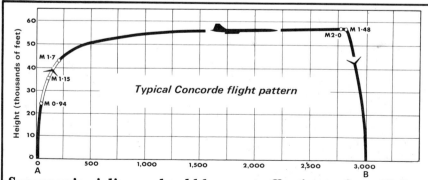

Typical Concorde flight pattern

Height (thousands of feet)

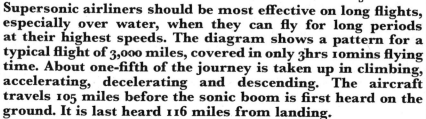

Supersonic airliners should be most effective on long flights, especially over water, when they can fly for long periods at their highest speeds. The diagram shows a pattern for a typical flight of 3,000 miles, covered in only 3hrs 10mins flying time. About one-fifth of the journey is taken up in climbing, accelerating, decelerating and descending. The aircraft travels 105 miles before the sonic boom is first heard on the ground. It is last heard 116 miles from landing.

For and against

Supersonic transports (SST's) are designed to fly passengers for thousands of miles, faster than the speed of sound. They are in production in Britain, France and Russia and the first planes came into service in 1976. Except in Russia, plans for SST's met fierce opposition, for many reasons. In America these caused Boeing's proposed SST to be cancelled before it was even built.

Because SST's are much more advanced than present-day slower-than-sound airliners, they were bound to present technical problems. Even before they had flown, their opponents said that they would be extremely noisy and would pollute the air (with dirt from their engines) more than other aircraft. However, many people believe that the British/French *Concorde* is no noisier than most existing jet airliners, and has much 'cleaner' engines than most of them. Work goes on all the time to make them quieter and cleaner still. What cannot be removed altogether is their 'sonic boom'. Because they fly faster than sound they produce a shock wave heard on the ground as a bang, so airlines have undertaken to fly at lower (subsonic) speeds over populated areas and avoid flying over land wherever this is possible. If the world's fuel situation gets worse, this too could affect their future, as they use much more than the slower jets.

The British-French programme

The *Concorde*, shown on the opposite page, is a joint programme, developed by both France and Britain. Teams in both countries designed and built it. These aircraft are so enormously expensive to develop that only the largest and richest countries could possibly afford to do it alone.

Supersonic airliners should, in general, be most effective on long range routes like those across the Atlantic, the Pacific, the North Pole or the vast unpopulated areas of Russia to the Far East. On these routes they would be able to keep up their supersonic speeds over great distances and cut existing journey times right down. The time for a flight from London to New York is little more than half of what it is on a supersonic jet.

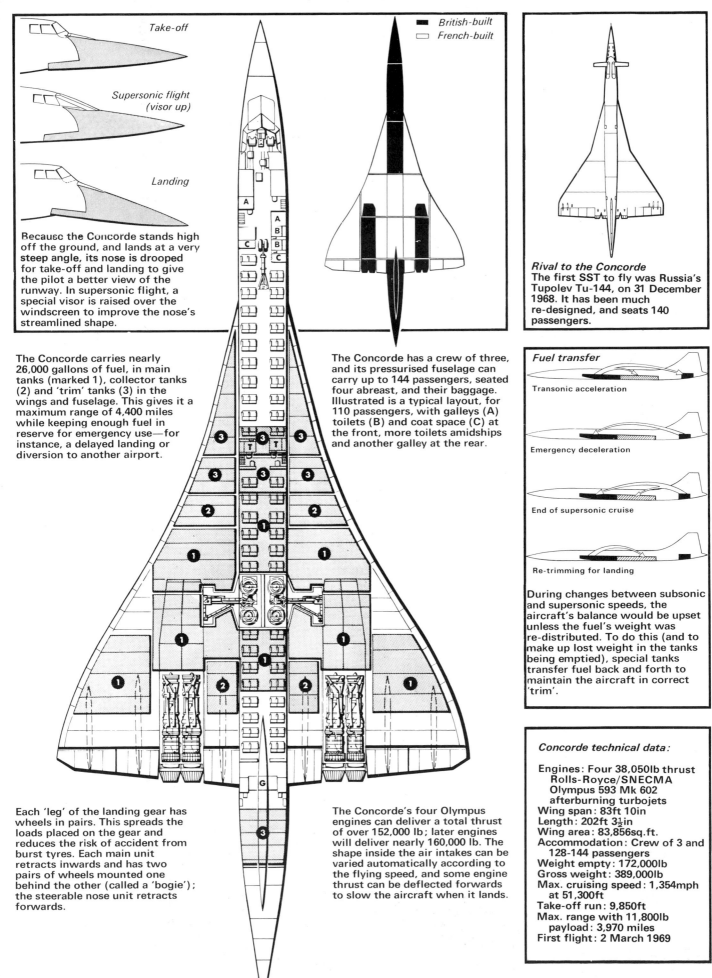

Take-off

Supersonic flight (visor up)

Landing

Because the Concorde stands high off the ground, and lands at a very steep angle, its nose is drooped for take-off and landing to give the pilot a better view of the runway. In supersonic flight, a special visor is raised over the windscreen to improve the nose's streamlined shape.

The Concorde carries nearly 26,000 gallons of fuel, in main tanks (marked 1), collector tanks (2) and 'trim' tanks (3) in the wings and fuselage. This gives it a maximum range of 4,400 miles while keeping enough fuel in reserve for emergency use—for instance, a delayed landing or diversion to another airport.

Each 'leg' of the landing gear has wheels in pairs. This spreads the loads placed on the gear and reduces the risk of accident from burst tyres. Each main unit retracts inwards and has two pairs of wheels mounted one behind the other (called a 'bogie'); the steerable nose unit retracts forwards.

■ *British-built*
□ *French-built*

The Concorde has a crew of three, and its pressurised fuselage can carry up to 144 passengers, seated four abreast, and their baggage. Illustrated is a typical layout, for 110 passengers, with galleys (A) toilets (B) and coat space (C) at the front, more toilets amidships and another galley at the rear.

The Concorde's four Olympus engines can deliver a total thrust of over 152,000 lb; later engines will deliver nearly 160,000 lb. The shape inside the air intakes can be varied automatically according to the flying speed, and some engine thrust can be deflected forwards to slow the aircraft when it lands.

Rival to the Concorde
The first SST to fly was Russia's Tupolev Tu-144, on 31 December 1968. It has been much re-designed, and seats 140 passengers.

Fuel transfer

Transonic acceleration

Emergency deceleration

End of supersonic cruise

Re-trimming for landing

During changes between subsonic and supersonic speeds, the aircraft's balance would be upset unless the fuel's weight was re-distributed. To do this (and to make up lost weight in the tanks being emptied), special tanks transfer fuel back and forth to maintain the aircraft in correct 'trim'.

Concorde technical data:

Engines: Four 38,050lb thrust Rolls-Royce/SNECMA Olympus 593 Mk 602 afterburning turbojets
Wing span: 83ft 10in
Length: 202ft 3½in
Wing area: 83,856sq.ft.
Accommodation: Crew of 3 and 128-144 passengers
Weight empty: 172,000lb
Gross weight: 389,000lb
Max. cruising speed: 1,354mph at 51,300ft
Take-off run: 9,850ft
Max. range with 11,800lb payload: 3,970 miles
First flight: 2 March 1969

Modern warplanes

America's *F-111* (right), built by General Dynamics, is the first operational warplane with 'swing-wing' design. Its wings are extended fully forward for take-off, low-speed flight and landing, but pivot back to a fully-swept position for high-speed flight. The F-111 can be used as a fighter, fighter-bomber and reconnaissance aircraft.

General Dynamics F-111A 1967

Designed as a two-seat carrier-borne bomber, the *Grumman A-6E Intruder* (right) can carry a huge load of bombs and attack missiles. It has very advanced radar, and a computer to help navigation and enable its weapons to be aimed accurately. A special four-seat version called the *Prowler* carries equipment to 'jam' or mislead enemy radar.

Grumman A-6E Intruder 1963

The *MiG-25* 'Foxbat' (right), which can fly at three times the speed of sound, is the fastest known Russian fighter and one of the fastest aircraft in the world. Because it can also fly at very great heights (80,000ft) it is used for high-speed photographic reconnaissance duties as well.

Mikoyan MiG-25 1962

America's most important new fighter, the *Eagle* (right), has two powerful jet engines, a rapid-firing multi-barrel gun, and can carry the latest air-to-air missiles. It was designed to be especially manoeuvrable in 'dog-fights' with other fighters, and can fly at more than twice the speed of sound.

McDonnell Douglas F-15 Eagle 1975

The Mirage

The French *Dassault Mirage III* is one of the most successful western warplanes of recent years. It was originally designed as a French all-weather fighter, but it has developed into a highly adaptable multi-purpose combat aircraft. About 1,200 *Mirage IIIs* have been ordered by air forces all over the world. The basic combat model is the *Mirage III-E*, versions of which have been built for France, Australia, Spain, Switzerland, South Africa, Pakistan, Brazil, Argentina, Venezuela, Zaïre and the Lebanon. There are also the *III-B* two-seat trainer, the *III-R* reconnaissance-fighter, the low-cost *Mirage 5*, the swept-wing *Mirage FI* and swing-wing *Mirage G8*.

Mirage 111-E technical data:
Engine: 13,670lb thrust Atar 9C afterburning turbojet
Wing span: 27ft
Length: 49ft 3½in
Wing area: 375sq.ft
Gross weight: 29,760lb
Max. speed: 1,460mph at 40,000ft
Time to 36,000ft: 3min
Typical combat radius: 745 miles

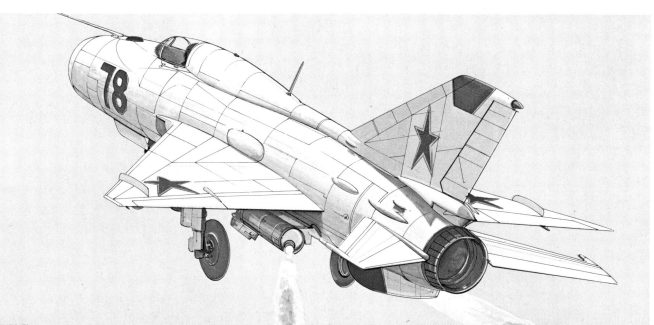

The MiG-21

Russia's *MiG-21* 'Fishbed', of which there are many versions, is rather less advanced than most western combat aircraft, but special-engine versions (E-66 and E-66A) have set world speed and height records of 1,484mph and 113,892ft.

The basic *MiG-21* is a short-range interceptor. Later models have better armaments and electronic equipment and can fight in all weathers. There are an enormous number of these fighters in service with about 20 air forces, including those of Russia, China, Czechoslovakia, Egypt, Finland, East Germany, India, Iraq, Poland, Syria and North Vietnam. There is a two-seater trainer version as well as a short-take-off experimental model.

MiG-21MF technical data:

Engine: 12,500lb thrust RD-13-300 afterburning turbojet
Wing span: 23ft 5½in
Length: 51ft 8½in
Wing area: 247 sq.ft
Gross weight: 20,725lb
Max. speed: 1,385mph at 36,000ft
Climb rate: 30,000ft per min
Typical combat radius: 375 miles

The Phantom American warplane of today

The large cutaway illustration on these two pages shows the F-4C, US Air Force two-seat fighter version of this multi-purpose warplane.

America's basic fighter

The *Phantom* is a multi-purpose combat aeroplane used widely by the US Navy and Air Force for many different jobs. It flew for the first time on 27 May 1958, and the first *Phantom* squadrons were formed late in 1960. More *Phantoms* have been built than any other American warplane since the Second World War; in 1974 the total had passed 4,300, with later models still in production.

Like many other modern warplanes, the *Phantom* can carry a wide variety of 'stores'—bombs, rockets, missiles or extra fuel tanks—under its wings and fuselage. The total weight of weapons which it can carry is greater than that carried by the four-engined heavy bombers of World War II; some typical loads are shown on the right. The naval versions, which serve on aircraft carriers, can fold their wings upwards so that they take up less space when they are stored in their hangars under the deck of the ship.

The *Phantom* can fly at nearly 2½ times the speed of sound, and can climb to a height of 60,000ft in less than 3 minutes.

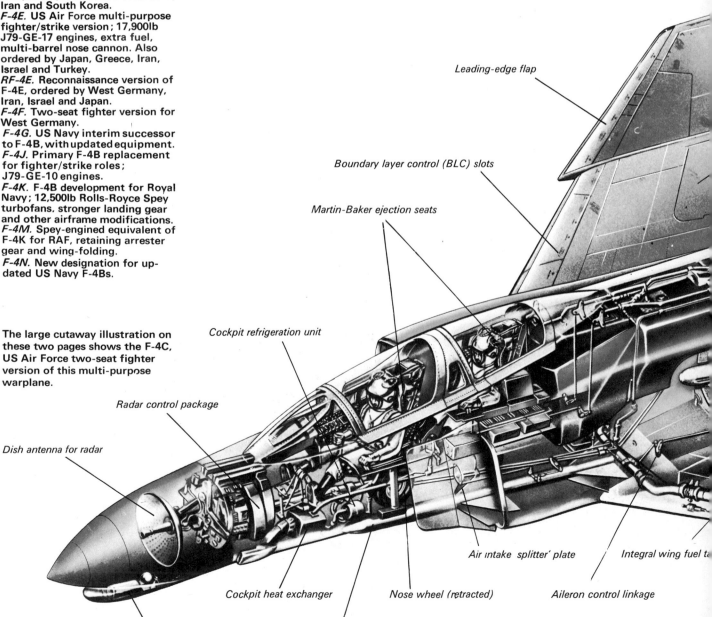

Leading-edge flap

Boundary layer control (BLC) slots

Martin-Baker ejection seats

Cockpit refrigeration unit

Radar control package

Dish antenna for radar

Infra-red target seeker

Cockpit heat exchanger

Semi-recessed Sparrow III missile

Nose wheel (retracted)

Air intake splitter' plate

Aileron control linkage

Integral wing fuel ta

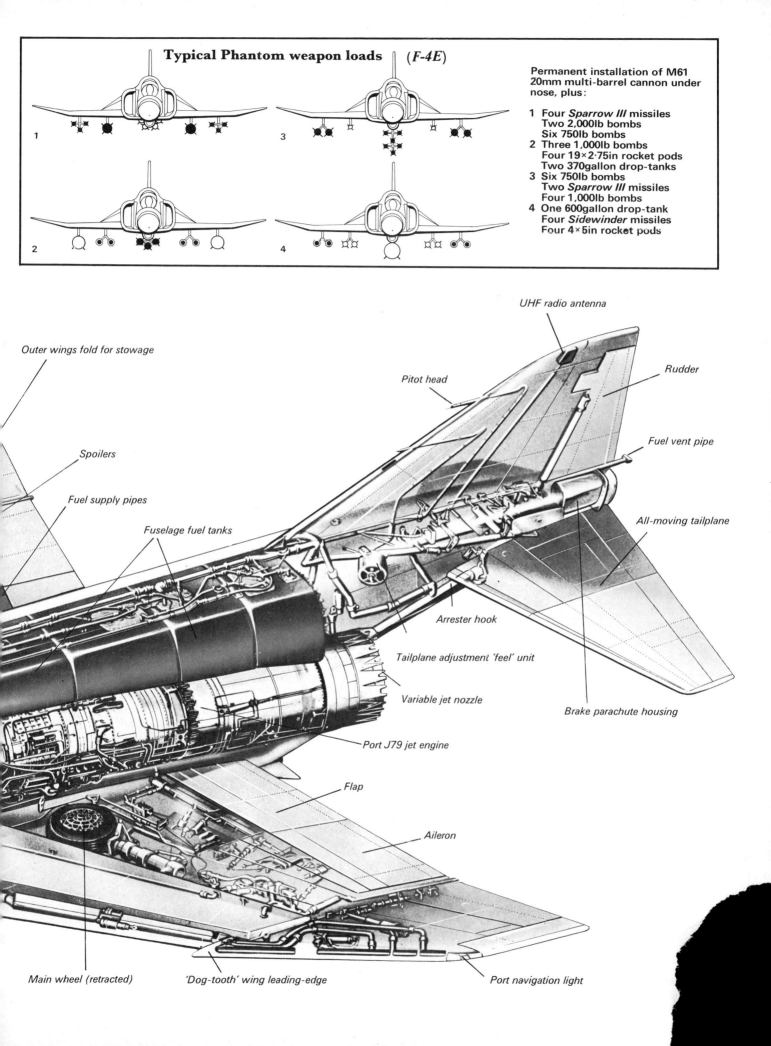

Typical Phantom weapon loads (*F-4E*)

1

2

3

4

Permanent installation of M61 20mm multi-barrel cannon under nose, plus:

1 Four *Sparrow III* missiles
  Two 2,000lb bombs
  Six 750lb bombs
2 Three 1,000lb bombs
  Four 19×2·75in rocket pods
  Two 370gallon drop-tanks
3 Six 750lb bombs
  Two *Sparrow III* missiles
  Four 1,000lb bombs
4 One 600gallon drop-tank
  Four *Sidewinder* missiles
  Four 4×5in rocket pods

Outer wings fold for stowage

Spoilers

Fuel supply pipes

Fuselage fuel tanks

UHF radio antenna

Pitot head

Rudder

Fuel vent pipe

All-moving tailplane

Arrester hook

Tailplane adjustment 'feel' unit

Variable jet nozzle

Brake parachute housing

Port J79 jet engine

Flap

Aileron

Main wheel (retracted)

'Dog-tooth' wing leading-edge

Port navigation light

VTOL vertical take-off and landing

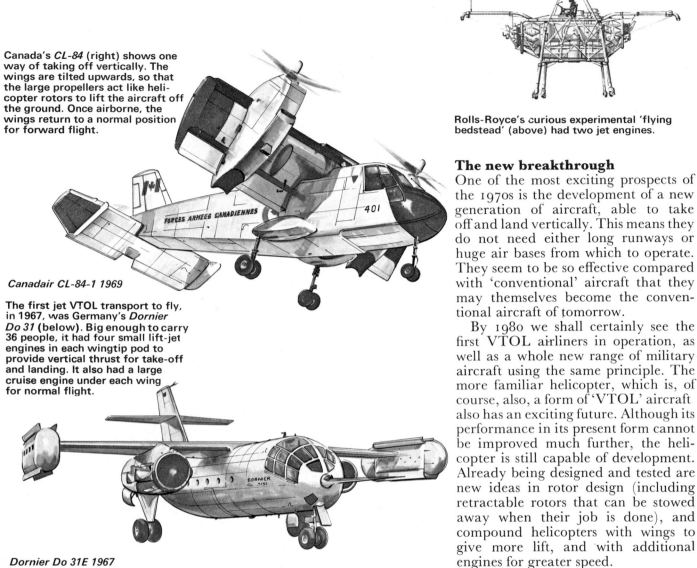

Canada's *CL-84* (right) shows one way of taking off vertically. The wings are tilted upwards, so that the large propellers act like helicopter rotors to lift the aircraft off the ground. Once airborne, the wings return to a normal position for forward flight.

Canadair CL-84-1 1969

The first jet VTOL transport to fly, in 1967, was Germany's *Dornier Do 31* (below). Big enough to carry 36 people, it had four small lift-jet engines in each wingtip pod to provide vertical thrust for take-off and landing. It also had a large cruise engine under each wing for normal flight.

Dornier Do 31E 1967

Rolls-Royce's curious experimental 'flying bedstead' (above) had two jet engines.

The new breakthrough

One of the most exciting prospects of the 1970s is the development of a new generation of aircraft, able to take off and land vertically. This means they do not need either long runways or huge air bases from which to operate. They seem to be so effective compared with 'conventional' aircraft that they may themselves become the conventional aircraft of tomorrow.

By 1980 we shall certainly see the first VTOL airliners in operation, as well as a whole new range of military aircraft using the same principle. The more familiar helicopter, which is, of course, also, a form of 'VTOL' aircraft also has an exciting future. Although its performance in its present form cannot be improved much further, the helicopter is still capable of development. Already being designed and tested are new ideas in rotor design (including retractable rotors that can be stowed away when their job is done), and compound helicopters with wings to give more lift, and with additional engines for greater speed.

The first fully-operational VTOL aeroplane, other than helicopters, was Britain's *Harrier* strike aircraft (right) which went into service in Britain in 1969, with the US Marines in 1971, and was later ordered by Spain. It has the unusual Rolls-Royce Bristol Pegasus engine, with exhaust gases which can be 'vectored' (deflected) through two movable nozzles on each side, to direct the thrust downward for take-off and landing and to intermediate positions during transfer between vertical and horizontal flight. This aeroplane can fly backwards and sideways as well as forwards, and carry 6,000lb of external ns.

Hawker Siddeley Harrier 1969

Boeing Vertol CH-47 Chinook 1962

Bell AH-1G HueyCobra 1967

Igor Sikorsky first flew his *VS-300,* the world's first practical helicopter, in 1939. Since then, this type of aircraft has gained a special place in aviation history. It can fly where fixed-wing aircraft cannot operate. Helicopters are specially useful for medical relief and rescue work. Recently, they have been used more and more for fighting as well. This picture shows a typical jungle battle area with helicopters doing three basic jobs: the *Bell HueyCobra* 'gunship', the *Iroquois* air ambulance and the *Boeing Vertol Chinook* assault transport.

Bell UH-1B Iroquois 1962

Gliders flying without engines

A typical single-seat glider is the British *Slingsby T.51 Dart* (right), of which several versions have been built since its first appearance in 1963. Darts gained 10 of the first 20 places in the 1967 British Gliding Championships. The construction is mainly of plywood and glass-fibre. The glider's gross weight is only 840lb. Its maximum speed (in smooth air) is 144mph.

Slingsby T.51 Dart 1963

The Czechoslovakian *Blanik* (right) is one of the world's most popular gliders. Well over a thousand have been built. It seats two people, one behind the other, and can perform aerobatics when flown solo or as a two-seater. Although it is capable of high-performance flying, it was designed basically as a trainer. A small engine can be fitted above the fuselage to enable the glider to take off without other assistance.

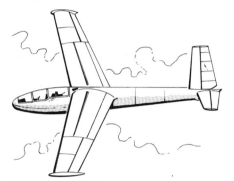
L-13 Blanik 1956

The Caproni Vizzola *A-21 Calif* (right). Among the most handsome modern gliders are the *Calif* series, designed and built by the famous Caproni company in Italy. They have done extremely well in gliding competitions, and have set up several new gliding records. One version has a tiny jet engine mounted in the lower fuselage, to enable it to take off without a towing aircraft or winch.

Caproni Vizzola A-21 Calif 1970

Flying without engines

The first aeroplanes to fly were of course gliders—that is, aeroplanes which had no motors but could only glide fairly slowly down to earth after having been launched from some high place. Then came the Wrights' historic breakthrough to powered flight, and the glider was almost forgotten. But after World War I, gliding was rediscovered as a sport, with new methods being discovered for long-distance flying, by using the currents in the air to gain height.

Gliding quickly became competitive, with pilots trying to see who could glide for the greatest distance across country. Since thermal up-currents (see opposite page), which make this possible, only rise strongly for about nine hours in the daytime, increased distances could only be covered by increasing speed. This led to the use of very long and narrow wings and greater streamlining.

In good conditions, modern gliders can travel for several hundred miles. The world distance record, set up in 1972, is 907 miles. Apart from trainers, which are usually designed for lower performance, modern gliders are divided broadly into two categories: the Standard Class—cheap, light, easy-to-fly gliders for club and private use, and the Open Class—very high performance gliders, suitable for competition flying.

There are three basic ways of getting a glider up into the air: pulling it up like a kite by means of a winch and cable, towing it up behind an aeroplane, or fitting it with a small engine for unassisted take-off.

The diagram on the right illustrates the first two of these methods. For a winch launch, the glider is attached by cable to a powerful winch, which pulls it along the ground until sufficient speed (about 50-60mph) and wing lift have been generated for it to leave the ground and go into a very steep climb. When it has climbed to about 200ft, the pilot levels out to begin his flight, at the same time releasing the launch cable which drops to the ground, ready for next launch.

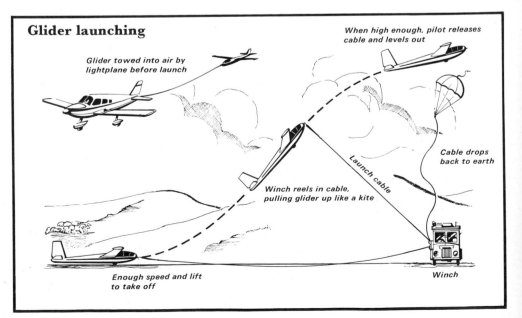

Glider launching

When high enough, pilot releases cable and levels out

Glider towed into air by lightplane before launch

Launch cable

Cable drops back to earth

Winch reels in cable, pulling glider up like a kite

Enough speed and lift to take off

Winch

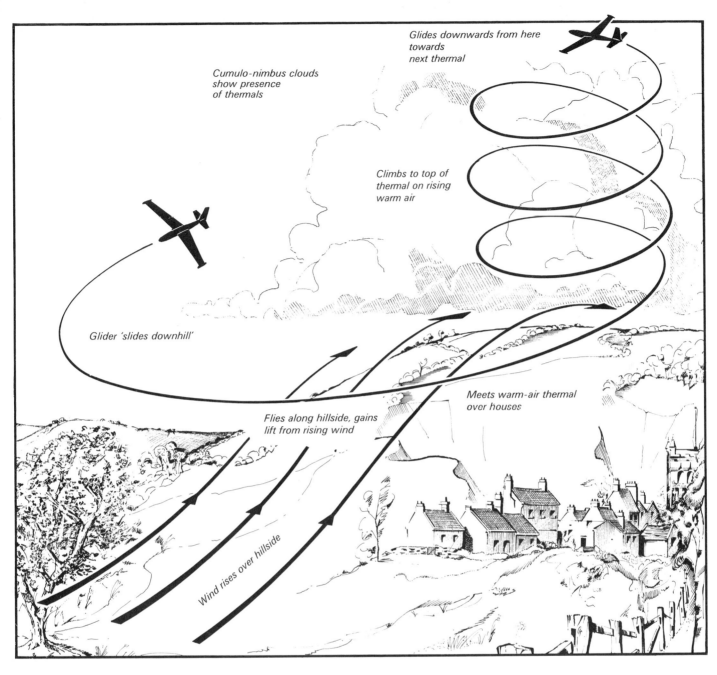

Glides downwards from here towards next thermal

Cumulo-nimbus clouds show presence of thermals

Climbs to top of thermal on rising warm air

Glider 'slides downhill'

Meets warm-air thermal over houses

Flies along hillside, gains lift from rising wind

Wind rises over hillside

How gliders gain height

Gliders have no engines to keep them up, although some have engines used only for take-off. They get their forward speed by 'sliding downhill' through the air. How, then, do they not only stay up in the air, perhaps for a hundred miles or more, but actually *gain* height?

There are two basic ways, both making use of upward-moving air currents: 'hill lift' and 'thermal convection'. 'Hill lift' occurs when wind blows against a hill and is forced upward. This was known and used by Lilienthal (see page 3) 80 years ago. It was not until the early 1920s that it was discovered that height could be kept up for longer periods by flying *along* a hillside instead of away from it.

The Austrian, Robert Kronfeld, pioneered the use of 'thermal convection' in gliding in 1928, when he discovered that warm up-currents of air usually produced certain types of cloud. Warm air, of course, is lighter than cool air, and therefore rises.

A rising column of warm air is called a 'thermal'. It is invisible, but it can be detected from the cloud patterns it makes. Above large towns air is almost always warmer too. And an instrument called a variometer (see right) tells a pilot when he is in an up-current. Having found a thermal, the glider pilot uses it to lift him in an ascending spiral until he reaches its top, when he again begins to 'slide downhill' again in search of the next thermal.

Altimeter   **Variometer**

Although he does not have fuel or engine instruments to worry about, the glider pilot does depend very much on two main instruments. One is the altimeter (above left), which records his height above the ground below. The other is the variometer (above right), a sensitive instrument designed speciall to measure how fast a glider is gaining, or losing, height.

What next? Experimental aircraft

Helicopters as we know them today cannot be made to fly much faster, but among ideas being studied is one to retract the rotors out of the way—into streamlined pods, as in this American project, or into the fuselage—when they are not wanted for take-off or landing.

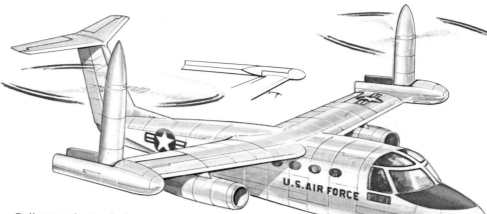

Bell stowed-rotor helicopter project

Several aircraft have been used in the US space programme. One machine designed for space work is the *Northrop HL-10* (right), officially called a 'lifting-body re-entry research vehicle'. Bigger 'space shuttle' machines like this will soon be able to fly out to orbiting space stations with supplies, return through the atmosphere and land on a runway like an ordinary aircraft.

Northrop HL-10

Man's age-old dream of flying by his own power, and not that of an engine, still continues. Sustained and controlled man-powered flight may yet be possible, perhaps in a machine like the Japanese *Linnet* (right). This has long-span wings like a glider and has already been flown for 300ft by a pilot pedalling furiously to turn the propeller.

Nihon Linnet III

DHC/Bell Buffalo ACLS test aircraft

One idea that could catch on for tomorrow's aircraft is to use an air-cushion landing system (ACLS), like that of a hovercraft, instead of a heavy, complicated metal undercarriage. The idea was being tested in America in the early 1970s on several aircraft, including this specially-modified Canadian Buffalo transport.

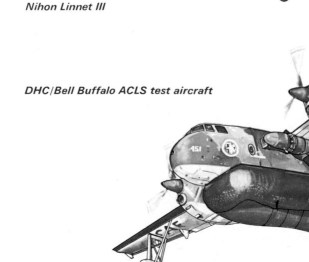

Projects supplement a simple glider

Aeromodelling is great fun. You can learn how and why an aeroplane flies by building and test flying your own models.

Start with a simple model, like the glider shown on this page. Flying model aeroplanes are always built of *balsa wood*, a light, strong wood specially cut in various standard sizes in sheet, strip and block form. Balsa can be glued with quick drying *balsa cement*. The wood should be cut to size and shape with a very sharp modelling knife. Use a steel ruler to make lines and cuts straight.

The design shown here is a simple glider with all-sheet balsa wings and tail surfaces. The fuselage is cut from a length of balsa strip. We have added all the control surfaces that a full-sized plane

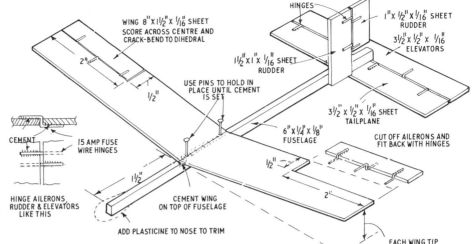

would have. These control surfaces are hinged in place with fuse wire or soft iron florists' wire, so that the various controls can be bent to

different positions to see what effect they have. A series of experiments is described and illustrated in the smaller diagrams below.

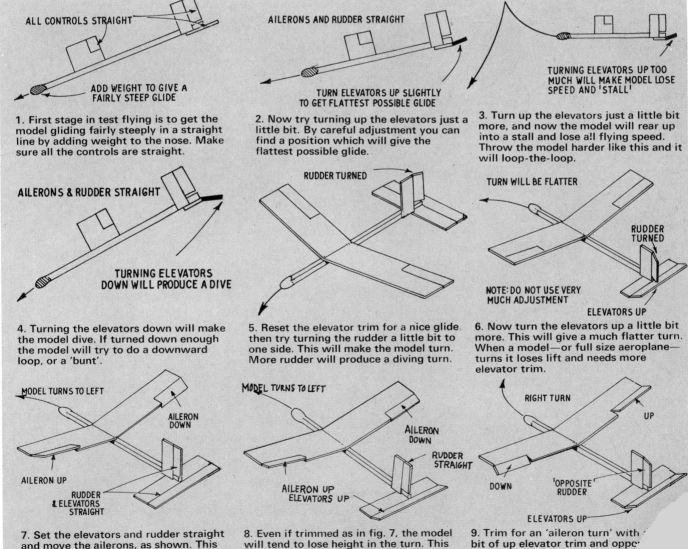

1. First stage in test flying is to get the model gliding fairly steeply in a straight line by adding weight to the nose. Make sure all the controls are straight.

2. Now try turning up the elevators just a little bit. By careful adjustment you can find a position which will give the flattest possible glide.

3. Turn up the elevators just a little bit more, and now the model will rear up into a stall and lose all flying speed. Throw the model harder like this and it will loop-the-loop.

4. Turning the elevators down will make the model dive. If turned down enough the model will try to do a downward loop, or a 'bunt'.

5. Reset the elevator trim for a nice glide, then try turning the rudder a little bit to one side. This will make the model turn. More rudder will produce a diving turn.

6. Now turn the elevators up a little bit more. This will give a much flatter turn. When a model—or full size aeroplane—turns it loses lift and needs more elevator trim.

7. Set the elevators and rudder straight and move the ailerons, as shown. This will also produce a turn, rather more gentle than a 'rudder turn'.

8. Even if trimmed as in fig. 7, the model will tend to lose height in the turn. This can be corrected by applying a little up elevator.

9. Trim for an 'aileron turn' with a bit of up elevator trim and opposite rudder. This should give the flattest of all.

Historic aircraft to make and fly

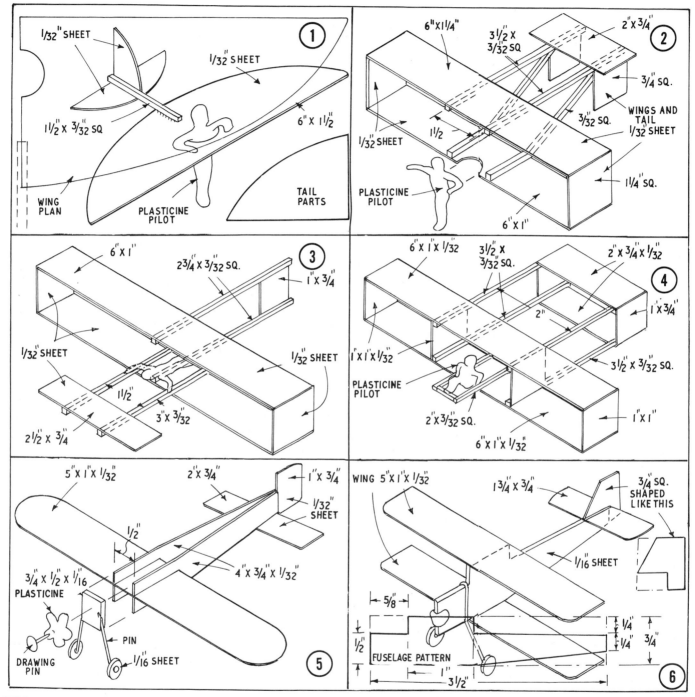

This page shows how to build several different kinds of model, each based on actual aircraft.

Some of the original *Lilienthal* gliders (**1**) had no tail surfaces, but you must fit a tail to get a model to [fly] properly. The plasticine 'pilot' [provi]des the trim weight.

[The] *Chanute* (**2**), *Wright* (**3**) and [...] (**4**) gliders have wings of [the]m—an upper and lower wing joined by small balsa panels at the tips. Cut these parts, to the dimensions given, from $\frac{1}{32}''$ sheet balsa. Cement together carefully taking care to get the complete wing square. Then cement on the $\frac{3}{32}''$ square spars, cut to the lengths shown, and add the tail parts cut from $\frac{1}{32}''$ sheet.

For the *Blériot* model (**5**), wing and tail parts are cut from $\frac{1}{32}''$ sheet.

Two fuselage sides are also cut from $\frac{1}{32}''$ sheet and slotted to take the wing. Add a nose former cut from $\frac{1}{16}''$ sheet.

For the *SE5* (**6**), the fuselage is cut to 'profile' shape from $\frac{1}{16}''$ sheet. Mark to the dimensions shown and cut out carefully. Wings and tail parts are cut from $\frac{1}{32}''$ sheet. Undercarriage legs can be bent from a straightened-out paper clip.

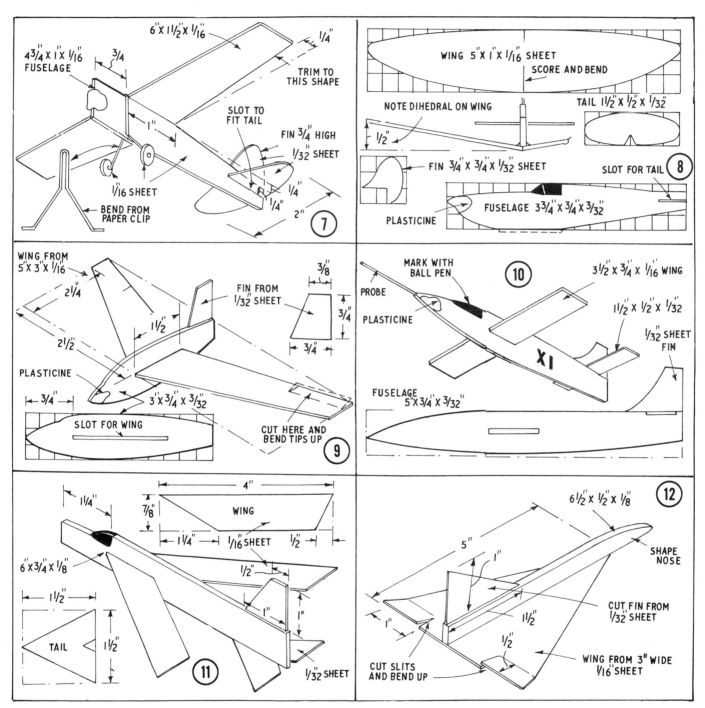

The *Vega* (**7**) monoplane had a thicker wing, so cut the wing from $\frac{1}{16}''$ sheet. Tail surfaces should have a curved outline shape, as shown.

Scale up the parts required for the *Spitfire* (**8**), using the $\frac{1}{4}''$ square grid. The Spitfire will need the wing crack-bending at the centre so that it can be given a *dihedral angle* when cemented to the bottom of the fuselage.

The *ME* 163 (**9**) has a fuselage slotted to take the swept back wing. Note how the wing shape is marked out on 3″ wide sheet.

The *Bell X-1* (**10**) has a small wing, so it will make a fast glider. You will probably find it a little bit more tricky to trim than some of the other models.

The *Lightning* (**11**) will also be a little bit tricky to get to fly properly.

It may, or may not, require plasticine nose weight. If it tries to roll, instead of fly level, bend up the rear of each wing an equal amount and add weight to the nose.

The *Delta* jet (**12**) should fly well with only a little trimming weight on the nose. Cutting slits in the rear edge of the wing and bending up to form 'elevons' is, however, very important.

Vertical take-off models

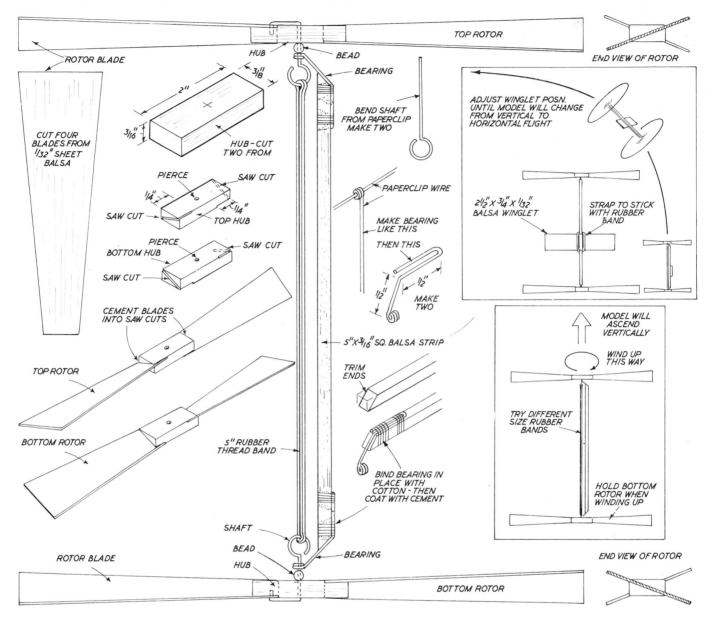

The model shown here is a simple helicopter. All parts are drawn actual size. Start by cutting out four rotor blades to the shape given from $\frac{1}{32}$" sheet balsa. Cut two hubs from $\frac{3}{8}$" $\times$ $\frac{3}{16}$" balsa strip. Using a saw, carefully make slots in each end of the hub at an angle running from edge to edge, as shown. Note that the angle of the slots is opposite at each end of the hub; and the angles on the bottom hub are the opposite way round to those on the top hub. When you have got these right, glue in the rotor blades with balsa cement.

The motor stick is a 5" length of $\frac{3}{16}$" square balsa strip. Trim off each end at an angle, as shown. Take two paper clips and straighten

them out. Use this wire to make two bearings, first bending the end into a small coil around a spare length of paper clip wire, then complete bending to proper shape. Bearings are bound to each end of the motor stick with cotton, followed by a generous coating of balsa cement.

The two shafts are also bent from straightened out paper clips. Pass the shaft through its bearing, slip on a small bead, and then push the rotor hub over the shaft. Turn the shaft over and back into the hub, using pliers, to complete the rotor assembly. Fit one rotor to each end of the motor stick. Now loop a thread band between the two shafts and your helicopter

model is ready to fly and demonstrate vertical flight.

Simply wind up the rubber band motor by hand, turning the top rotor and holding the bottom rotor still. Hold the stick and release both rotors, which will then rotate in opposite directions. Release the stick and the model should climb vertically upwards. Experiment with different sizes of rubber bands.

Now add a winglet to the motor stick. This time the model should start to climb vertically, then gradually turn over until it is flying sideways. Try adjusting the position of the winglet until you can get the model to change from vertical flight to true horizontal flight.

Index

Metric conversion table

1 in = 25.4 mm
1 ft = 0.3 m
1 mile = 1.6 km

1 sq ft = 0.09 sq m

1 lb = 0.45 kg